"I have known walked through "Along that one whose demeanor screamed ... confident, and talented woman of God that she is today. It goes without saying that I endorse Georgia and now herein recommend this book as a blueprint, based in scripture and validated by real life experiences, for those who want to overcome."

—*Kenneth W. Bangs*, D.Min.

"Georgia Smith is a precious friend that labored in love over *You Are My Beloved, Now Believe It*. Like Georgia, it is a prophetic dance that will captivate your emotions and grip your mind.

"*You Are My Beloved, Now Believe It* is a rich and compelling story of Georgia's journey into the heart of our bridegroom, Jesus, overlaid in the story of Song of Solomon. She has aptly painted a picture of her discovery of the love of God, herself and others through this remarkable tale of overcoming heartbreak and betrayal. The revelation that she shares from the Song of Solomon creates a canvas of art that you can join. I encourage you to read this book. It is not only compelling but will transform your understanding of the nature, personality, and extravagant love of Christ."

—Tracy Eckert, Director, HOZ
Dallas, Texas

"Georgia is a woman with a unique combination of talent and heart. Her counseling endeavors to encourage, heal, and transform the lives of others are a good "tell" about her inner health. I have witnessed her authentic love of life and people and affirm she has found and applied foundational truths of the ages that enable a real and vibrant life. In her book *You Are My Beloved, Now Believe It*, Georgia sagely walks us through the discovery of these truths. She weaves her personal journey in applying them to her own life and addresses relevant issues of hardships and how to deal with them. She has a calling to enable others to "live life and not just tolerate it," and this book is a profound tool to enable others do just that!"

—Thomas Waddle
Pres. Thomas Construction Management Company

"As followers of Christ, it is very important that we know the love of the Father and receive a greater revelation of His love for us. Georgia leads us through the Song of Solomon, which is a beautiful picture of how much Christ loves His bride. I believe you will enjoy the journey of learning to know God's love in a greater way as you read her book."

—Pastor Terry Moore
Sojourn Church, Carrollton, Texas

"*You Are My Beloved, Now Believe It* captured me as few books have. A multifaceted revelation of Christ and His love for us flows from Georgia's pen bringing comfort to us – His creation. An understanding of that love has taken me to a deeper communion with the Beloved. This is a book not just of information but one of transformation."

—Trudy Bangs
Nehemiah Prayer Network

YOU ARE
MY BELOVED,
NOW **BELIEVE IT**

*Debbie —
You are
His beloved —
Because of Him,
George*

Table of Contents

Foreword 11
Take a Walk with Me 13
   Let's Get Personal 15
A Word to Men 23
He Is Perfect 25
At the Core of His Heart 43
   Relentless Love 46
Who Are You? 55
   I Am a Lily 57
   You Are My Fairest One 60
Love's Delayed Response 81
Draw Me Away with You 85
   September 4, 2011 87
   Personal Vision 89
Beauty for Ashes 93
A Time of Waiting 97
Catch Us the Little Foxes 107
A Seal Fashioned from Love
   and Covered in Grace 113

Foreword

> *...And the dragon was enraged with the woman, and he went to make war with the rest of her offspring, who keep the commandments of God and have the testimony of Jesus Christ.* (Revelation 12:17 NKJV)

Life is tough, period. But it is a literal war for those who choose to keep the commandments of God and have the testimony of Jesus.

We all need a source from which we can draw encouragement, the strength needed to pass through the valley of the shadow in which we all must walk, and the balm of pure love to heal the wounds of life. Thus the value, product, and purpose of the Song of Solomon, the sole surviving work of his 1005 songs.

Here is a love song illustrative of the wooing, the winning, and the heartaches of wedded love. It speaks of the ultimate love between man and woman (eros) and of the spiritual love of God for His people (agape) and Jesus for His church (sacrificial).

If one accepts the premise that the root word of music is muse, and that muse in its purest sense refers to spirit, then it becomes obvious that man needs to exercise caution relative to the music he allows to access his inner most being.

The Spirit of a song can encourage one's heart, soothe one's pain, and renew one's walk in purpose.

Perfect in illustrating the Restorative Spirit of this Song of Songs is the life of Georgia Smith. Her walk has been challenging, her pain deep. Yet resident in her heart is the understanding that she is created for a purpose by the keeper of her Spirit.

Georgia rejected the opportunity to surrender to the pain of abuse, the hopelessness that comes with betrayal by one's wedded love and the enemy's lie that she was lesser than, to become the explication of the scriptural declaration…*I can do all things through Christ who strengthens me…*

Deep in the lonely nights Georgia sought God. His word penned so passionately by Solomon rekindled the fires of a heart starved for affirmation of her desirability and value.

She feasted on the passion of His love for her. She came to see that indeed she was lovely, not just physically, but as His *Spiritual Bride*. As her understanding of His word grew, so did her resolve to overcome. And she has.

The proof lies herein. Read it as it is meant to be read… with ardor, with expectation and with an open heart.

—Kenneth W. Bangs, D.Min.

Take a Walk with Me

Life is a journey. I am learning to enjoy the steps along the way, to savor the special moments life brings, and to not get in too big a hurry to reach my destiny. If we will take the time to focus our hearts on the moments and not the end, we will see more clearly truths of God's divine character and love. We will experience His love in real ways we have never realized before. The end result is very important because we must have a purpose and a vision or we will roam aimlessly without direction. But there are many truths and joys along the way to be cherished. We must allow Him to take hold of our hearts and minds, focusing on the moments of life each day. The results are more thankful and joyful hearts, clarity, purpose, and divine revelations from Him. It has taken me half a lifetime to realize this simple truth. Because of this truth, a very special journey for me began. I pray you savor and enjoy, even soak in the pages of this book. It's a look into my soul. I want you to walk with me on my journey. My purpose for writing this book is that as you gaze into my journey, your journey will become more real and evident.

While on a short trip at International House of Prayer in Kansas City in 2005, the Lord impressed upon me the idea about writing this book. He gave me the title, and that was all. I pondered that He is actually called the Beloved in the Song of Solomon. So why would He want me to title the book in a way that would call us a beloved as well when that's the word to describe Him. For the last five years, I have poured over this beautiful, descriptive book of love, yet never completely understood why He calls us His beloved instead of another qualifying word for us until now! You see, the reason is that as we gaze our eyes upon Son of God and begin to see ourselves as He sees us, we truly become more like Him and our names become the same: beloved.

During that time in Kansas City, I was going through much healing in my life. I had been married for twenty-seven years and only recently divorced for two years, and was still healing from hurt, trying to let God show me who I was and what He thought of me. I was on a quest for my identity. I wanted to know what God thought about me and what He had to say about me. I wanted to know why I was created and would He bring some usefulness from all the hurt, pain, and chaos I felt for so many years. Trust me, there were times that were wonderful and beautiful in the twenty-seven years of my marriage. But even before my marriage, my life had been filled with disappointment after disappointment and chaos. I have walked securely with the Lord since April 1984, but not without hardship and some difficulty. If it had not been for the Beloved's sustaining love and hand upon my life, I would have given up.

LET'S GET PERSONAL

I am a mother of three beautiful children, who are grown now. Some of the best years of my life were spent being a young mom attending to all their special functions and sports activities. I loved helping them and felt so needed. I felt I had a place in this world. I understood my place in their lives and the importance I played on a daily basis. This time in my life taught me that being a perfect mom is unattainable, but making sure your children know how much they are loved is attainable. My children absolutely know that I love them. I prayed daily for them and for what God had in store for their destinies. Even though their father and I did not continue being married, we both truly love our children. It was an extremely difficult marriage, but I will not go into that at this point. Needless to say, the sadness and hurt was overwhelming when our lives took a turn toward divorce. Divorce is horrible, and I believe it should be avoided at all cost if possible. Although this was a very difficult time, I saw God's loving hand upon my life and my loved ones' lives.

Twenty-seven years is a very long time to be married. The twenty-two years prior to the married years were just as difficult and dysfunctional. I remember that as a little girl, one of the desires of my heart was to have a happy home with a husband who loved me. I dreamed of the perfect family. Little girls and boys believe that life will offer the best unless they are put in situations over and over that cause their dreams and hopes to be shattered. Deferred hope is an epidemic in the hearts of many people. Deferred hope would render us crippled with no vision of our purpose and destiny along our journey, but because of Christ's loving encounter with His truth about our purpose and destiny we have assured hope of fulfilling our purpose.

My view of life, hope, and dreams were tested at a very young age. I am the third child of four children. I have a half sister and half brother older than me. I am the firstborn from my father and have a younger biological brother. My mother and father met and became pregnant with me. They had anticipated aborting me and were on their way to do so when they decided not to and instead got married. I learned about their decision to keep me when I was thirteen. I must say I was very thankful they suddenly changed their minds, and there are many days I have thanked God for moving their hearts and allowing me to be born. Our destinies and lives are truly in His hands. But of course, they did not know each other well, and my father did what he felt was best and right for me and my mother. As a result, their marriage began with difficulties and adjustments. My mother had been married and divorced previously before meeting my father. My half sister and half brother were very young when they married, ages three and two. The four of us grew up together and were very close. My mother was an extremely smart woman with lots of natural athletic ability. She no longer is with us, but I know she is with the Lord and is enjoying every minute being in heaven. I want to honor her in her death as well as in her life. So what I am about to reveal is not meant to discredit her in any way. Revealing the truth about my childhood is only meant to help every person reading this book get a better glimpse of the Heavenly Father's love. You see, if God can put His finger on me and mold me into the person He planned me to be, then He can do so for any life.

My mother was not a very maternal mom. She took care of her children, but in many ways, I believe she was not challenged enough and was bored. She also did not feel completely loved by my father, but mainly she felt he married her more out of obligation than love. It was difficult for her to feel loved by him for many reasons. She would take this frustration out on her children, especially my older half sister and half brother. The home was filled with tension. She became very unhappy and depressed on many occasions where she did not want to be alive. She attempted to take her life but failed. God loved her and knew we needed her. It wasn't time for her to go. I remember that as a little girl of about five years old, I would hide all possible items in the home that my mother might use to hurt herself. I loved my mom and wanted to protect her. I believe my brothers and sister felt the same way. The tension and fighting between my mom and dad grew worse over time, and there were things said and done that should never happen in a home. My father could have been a better husband and done many things different to have helped her, but I believe at that time he did the best he knew.

My refuge came in the summers when my younger brother and I spent time with our grandparents. My grandparents were some of the most wonderful people I will ever have had the honor of knowing. I learned much about love, friendship, prayer, kindness, and family spending summertime with them. I have many happy memories. My grandparents became my role models and had it not been for them, I'm not sure where I would be today. I'm thankful I had such wonderful grandparents to fill the voids that were lacking in my home life.

I grew up always wanting to obey and make my parents proud. I wanted to please. I was a smart little girl and could make friends easily. I had a strong sense of responsibility at a young age. I was a very good student in school until the ninth grade, which took a spiral downward after my parents' divorce. Usually when parents divorce, the mother and father share in the responsibility of the children. In my case, my mother was asked to leave by my father, which she did reluctantly, and my father became the parent who cared for us all of the time. I can only imagine what was going through her mind having to leave her children—she felt she had very little choice in the situation. I do believe she felt it was best for everyone that she leave the family.

So the quest and journey to birth this book actually began a very long time ago but was made absolutely clear I was to write in Kansas City in 2005 while I was there. During the time in Kansas City I began to study the book of Song of Solomon. I had always loved reading the Song of Solomon and thought it was beautiful but did not completely understand it. I knew enough about it to know that it is a true love story. I began to put some understanding to the symbolism in this beautiful love story, Song of Solomon—the love story of the Beloved longing for His perfect and beautiful bride, the Shulamite.

The name *Shulamite* means perfect one, peaceable one, and pacified. In the Song of Solomon the Shulamite represents each and every person who loves the Beloved, or Christ. The Beloved calls those who love Him a beloved because they begin to take on His identity and character as seen in the chapters that unfold the story of love. The meaning of beloved refers to an intimate relationship of love. This relationship is the greatest love story ever told. Over the course of the last six years, I have studied, meditated on this book and even taught others what God was showing me about true love that can be mysterious and yet simple, pure and satisfying to the core, always perfectly unconditional. It has become my favorite book of the Bible because of the healing it has brought to me. I can see myself from His eyes now and know more why I was created. My prayer as you read this book is that you are touched by His love as the pages unfold this truth and that your identity will be unraveled piece by piece as you begin your journey to healing, restoration, value, identity, destiny, and above all else, satisfaction; knowing at the depth of your being that someone loves you far more than you can possibly comprehend. In fact, that someone named Jesus wants to spend the rest of your time on earth and eternity gazing at you and being overcome by your beauty and strength. He is in you and you are in Him… in His perfectly abiding love.

When love finds you, it takes on special moments to make sure you are convinced it is real and lasting. One day, a few years ago, I was feeling lonely and a bit forgotten. This was one of those days when I needed a little something extra to reassure me that He still thinks I'm the apple of His eye even though I had a knowledge of Jesus' love for me. As long as I live on this earth, I will continue to want that reassurance. Jesus, on the other hand, wants to always make His love known to us and is overtaken with a lovesick heart when we express our emotions for Him. While driving in my car on this special day when loneliness struck my soul, I happened to notice the sign on the back window of the car in front of mine. Before I saw this painted sign, I had asked the Lord to show me in some way or tell me just how special I am. I know His word declares it, but sometimes I want something to be shown to me in the simplicity of everyday life. I needed an ah-ha moment. So when I looked at the back of this car, I saw that the painted sign was of a small child kneeling down facing the cross, with her hands lifted up toward the sky. And on each side of her, a little lower than her arms, were the words "Daddyz Girl." Tears formed in my eyes, and a moment of awe and lovesick warmth struck me at the very core of my being. I knew it was one of those special but very simple moments in time in my life that Jesus had heard my cry and prayer and was determined to speak to me through the sign on the back of that car. That very special moment in my journey is unforgettable and extremely impactful to my soul knowing He loves us, sees us and hears our cries always. We are always on His mind.

My hope and prayer is that as you read this book and as your journey begins with more awareness of His incredible and overflowing love, you will be overtaken by many of these moments and encounters along the way. The Lord is just waiting to unfold thoughts, plans, and feelings for you in ways you have never known. Get excited and be ready for an encounter with the Lover of your soul, Jesus.

Prayer: Beloved, I ask you to encounter me on my journey and reveal yourself as the Lover of my soul. I want to know your thoughts and plans for me. I desperately need to know how much you love me. Let my journey now begin to be our journey together. In Jesus's name, Amen.

A Word to Men

Men, much of the symbolisms in the Song of Solomon, when speaking of the Shulamite, appears very feminine. The Shulamite is symbolic of Christ's church. The Beloved represents Christ's attributes and characteristics. We are all the Father's beloved children, and we are all the brides of Christ, both male and female. Women, as well as men, are called the sons of God and warriors. Men, as well as women, are called the bride of Christ. I want to encourage you to read this book with a heart to capture the meaning of the message and not allow yourself to get bogged down with the gender and symbolisms that appear so feminine.

As you read the next chapter, "He Is Perfect," allow yourself to identify with His perfect and flawless nature. Men, if you desire to become a man like Christ, allow His character to change you to become more like Him. Notice what Christ the Beloved says and does toward the Shulamite. Notice the incredible encouragement, protection, and desire He has for her. Everything He says and does flows out of pure love, and He desires these same qualities to become your qualities too. God desires women to have Christ attributes as well. So, ladies, pay attention to all descriptions of the Beloved that the Shulamite expresses.

It is important for male and female readers of this book to focus on the characteristics and love flowing between both the Shulamite and the Beloved, realizing that they are a perfect picture together of love—the Beloved's love being perfectly mature and the Shulamite's love in the process of maturing. Identify where you are and where you want to be in the pages of this book as well as in the Scriptures. You most likely will identify with many aspects of this book while considering your own journey. You are here in many different seasons of your life. Take hold of the treasures that speak to your heart, remembering that His love is covering you, and we all are His beloved ones.

> ***Prayer:*** Beloved, I know the Song of Solomon is a love story written to convey Christ's love and purpose for me. Show me whatever you want to reveal about your love. Help me to keep my mind and heart open to hear what you have to say about who I am. Whether I am a woman or man, I know your love for us is the same. I want to understand more about how you see me. In Jesus's name, Amen.

HE IS PERFECT

When Perfect Love's true character and identity are revealed, we can see our true character and identity much clearer because we are a reflection of Him. My beloved, do you believe this?

In the beginning of Song of Solomon, the Shulamite meets the Beloved and is mesmerized by His words and affirmation of her. Song of Solomon 1:2, 4 says, "Let him kiss me with the kisses of his mouth—for your love is better than wine…Draw me away!" The Shulamite is longing for a close relationship with her Beloved where she can hear what He says about her. She desperately needs and wants to know her true identity, and she understands He is the one that can express this to her as she affirms that His "love is better than wine," meaning the things of the world weigh nothing compared to what her Beloved says and feels toward her! She knows her life depends on Him more than anything the world has to offer.

The Shulamite then begins in honesty revealing her own thoughts about herself when she states, "I am dark, but lovely, O daughters of Jerusalem, like the tents of Kedar, like the curtains of Solomon; do not look upon me because I am dark, because the sun has tanned me. My mother's sons were angry with me; they made me the keeper of the vineyards, but my own vineyard I have not kept" (Song of Solomon 1:5–6). The Shulamite admits that the cares of the world and sin have darkened her life in these verses. Tents of Kedar were covered in black goats' skins, and the curtains of Solomon were woven in dark threads. She has cared more about pleasing others and tending to what has been expected of her than tending to her own heart (vineyard). She has neglected her own life (vineyard) at the expense of others. She gave herself to other's agenda and has accomplished things in her own strength. The neglect of her own life has brought her to a crossroads in desperation to find her true identity. As she is on this journey to find her identity, she is surprised with an encounter of Perfect Love, the Beloved. Song of Solomon 1:7 says, "Tell me, O you whom I love, where you feed your flock, where you make it rest at noon. For why should I be as one who veils herself by the flocks of your companions?" She wants to come closer to Him and others He cares for. She knows she will find rest in His company. She no longer wants to be an outsider and veil herself, but she wants to belong in His company of companions: those whom He loves and who loves Him. She sees a rest and provision that she has never seen before. She is ready to separate herself from the ones who have wounded her and cared little for her—those whose love is shallow and worldly.

The Beloved knows the Shulamite seeks her place of rest and companionship so He directs her path, declaring, "If you do not know, O fairest among women, follow in the footsteps of the flock, and feed your little goats beside the shepherds' tents" (Song of Solomon 1:8). He not only is calling her to come into the fellowship with the others whom He loves but He asks her to bring those whom she cares for and loves with her, the flocks that she is responsible for. He also begins to declare to her how He sees her and what His thoughts are about her in verses nine and ten: "I have compared you, my love, to my filly among Pharaoh's chariots. Your cheeks are lovely with ornaments, your neck with chains of gold." Pharaoh obtained the finest of animals to carry his chariot. Nothing less than the best would do, so the Beloved declares this likeness to her. A filly is considered lively, high-spirited, and young. The Shulamite is young in her understanding of who she is, but she is excited and ready to learn more about who the Beloved is and His love for her. She knows it is the key to her true identity. Her cheeks represent her emotions, and the ornaments represent her choices. The Beloved is pleased with her heart's emotion to follow Him. He affirms her choice and assures her that as she follows in the right path toward Him, her authority will be one of great value and strength, which represent chains of gold around her neck.

As He speaks to her about who she is, His true love and identity begins to unfold. She declares, "While the king is at his table, my spikenard sends forth its fragrance. A bundle of myrrh is my Beloved to me, that lies all night between my breasts. My beloved is to me a cluster of henna blooms in the vineyards of En Gedi" (vv. 12–14). Spikenard is an expensive perfume used by Mary of Bethany to anoint Christ's head and feet before His death. It was her life savings. Because she considers the Beloved a king in her eyes, the Shulamite proclaims her desire to do the same for the Beloved. She carries Him close to her heart at all times. His actions and statements state a life of royalty and are comparable to the beautiful fragrance and beauty of the henna blooms in En Gedi, an extremely fertile and beautiful region.

Their conversation continues, declaring and proclaiming strong emotion and affirmation. He then states in Song of Solomon 1:15, "Behold, you are fair, my love! Behold, you are fair! You have dove's eyes." He begins to let her know how beautiful she is inside and out. A dove's eyes do not move, so if a dove wants to glance in another direction, it must turn its entire head in that direction. The Beloved tells the Shulamite how He has noticed her focused attention upon Him. When she continues to focus on Him only, she becomes a reflection of Him. Her identity is being revealed more and more to her as she continues to set her gaze only in His direction. Her awareness of His character increases. She proclaims, "Behold, you are handsome, my Beloved! Yes, pleasant! Also our bed is green. The beams of our houses are cedar, and our rafters of fir. I am the rose of Sharon, and the lily of the valleys" (Song of Solomon 1:16–17, 2:1). It is His inner character that is so handsome. She sees how He will protect her and how enjoyable their relationship is becoming. It is pleasant, and life is springing forth from their communication with each other as represented by the color green. The boundaries and foundation of her life is secure as represented by the strength of cedar for beams and the fir for overhead covering. She is feeling more secure and safe in His protection, knowing that whatever may come her way, the foundation they are building will remain strong and secure. As reassurance in who He is increases, so does her identity as she proclaims that she is "the rose of Sharon and the lily of the valleys." This rose is very special and unique in that when it blooms, its beauty is breathtaking; it is considered the most beautiful flower in all the valleys. He knows just what she needs to become all that destiny has determined for her.

> The voice of my beloved! Behold, he comes leaping upon the mountains, skipping upon the hills. My beloved is like a gazelle or a young stag. Behold, he stands behind our wall; He is looking through the windows, gazing through the lattice. My beloved

spoke, and said to me: "Rise up, my love, my fair one and come away. For lo, the winter is past, the rain is over and gone. The flowers appear on the earth; the time of singing has come, and the voice of the turtledove is heard in our land. The fig tree puts forth her green figs, and the vines with the tender grapes give a good smell. Rise up, my love, my fair one, and come away! "O my dove, in the clefts of the rock, in the secret places of the cliff, let me see your face, let me hear your voice. For your voice is sweet, and your face is lovely."

—Song of Solomon 2:8–14

In the gentle stillness of His voice (1 Kings 19:12), He is calling her and requesting that she comes away with Him. He knows her only hope for fulfillment and meaning in her life is if she will go with Him wherever He calls her. She knows He must rescue her and encounter the mountains and hills in her life. The Beloved begins His request for her to come away with Him by "leaping upon the mountains and hills" in her life—those things that keep her from Him. Anything that is trying to come between the two of them is a mountain or a hill. Distractions, relationships, sin, idolatry, wounds that are not healed, generational curses that need to be broken, and unhealthy soul ties are all mountains. Do you know what your mountains are that you want Him to leap upon and crush? Let the

Beloved reveal to you anything in your life that keeps you at a distance from Him. As He leaps upon those things that cause distance, they are crushed only to form more of His character in you. And so His strength becomes evident as He leaps upon the hindrances of her life. She describes Him to be like a "gazelle or young stag." Have you ever observed the strength and grace of a gazelle or young stag in their surroundings? They are magnificently endowed with agility and power. The power and grace they display when they leap and run declares freedom and assurance in their steps. Their gait is purposeful. If you watch them long enough, you begin to feel their power. It makes you want to run with them! Take a moment to stop and journal what He brings to your mind. Allow Him to bring the healing you need in your life through prayer and reading Scriptures. Ask the Beloved simply what the next step is you should take toward wholeness. He will destroy those mountains that keep you from feeling more of His love in your heart. Let Him into the chambers of your heart you have closed off from anyone. You may not want to look into those chambers because it feels painful or shameful and it leaves you feeling condemned or as a failure. But He is the perfect one who does not condemn, betray, or reject. His only true purpose is to love you and draw you closer to Himself ever so gently.

What about the walls, windows, and lattice that this Scripture mentions? The Beloved leaps upon the mountains and the hills, but He stands at the wall, peering through the window and lattice. Walls you have erected to keep the Beloved and others out He will not walk through or tear down unless invited to do so because the Beloved is a gentlemen. This is the way of love. Although force will not be used to help you see, He will allow enough pressure to be exerted over the circumstances and experiences in your life to bring you to a place of acknowledging the old hurts and behaviors that need attention before you can move forward. Take note of the Beloved's priestly quality. He is ever mindful of what you need to see, more than you realize, and the Beloved loves you enough to help you get to a place of complete awareness of what needs to be tended to in your life. What walls have you put up to keep Him out? Are they walls of false protection because you have been hurt over and over when your heart was so free to love? Walls of false protection can feel like unemotional expression or coldness. These walls mask themselves in fear of emotional intimacy. Pushing someone away or abandoning them first in fear they will abandon you is a manifestation of a wall. These walls can also be masked in fear of trusting others enough to be yourself around them and reveal your innermost struggles and thoughts. Fear of being accepted and loved for who you are is a wall of bondage and needs to be removed. These walls of false protection appear in many different forms and expressions. Allow the Beloved to show you what they are in your life. Freedom to be who He created you to be is beyond these walls.

The Beloved builds stones of remembrance from difficulties in our lives that only He can move. In these places of hardship we meet Him because there is no one else who can meet us in those places like He can. The Beloved crosses over and leaps on places in our lives that are impassable except by Him.

He speaks to us in so many different ways—through Scriptures, through nature, through the still and small voice, through impressions, through dreams and visions, through others, through the silence, and through music and the arts. But are we aware? Are we really listening and expecting such a wonderful and powerful God to take time and speak to man? The truth is, the Beloved cannot wait to speak because there is such an overwhelming love in His heart for us. Intense desire and passion for the ones created in His own image compels the Beloved to express His thoughts and love to them at any given moment.

The Beloved calls us to come away with Him. He desires our undivided attention, but understands we have work that must be done here on earth. The Beloved also knows that in order to really understand Him and ourselves better, He must draw us near and we must respond spending that time with Him, devoted and unhindered by distractions of the world. In Song of Solomon 2, the Beloved is calling his love to "rise up and come away with Me, my fair one, my love." Will we respond to His voice?

Do you remember falling in love for the first time and how important it was to spend time with the one who captured your heart? You knew the only way to know each other was to spend special moments of your life together. So it is with Him. The Beloved is such the perfect pursuer, always wanting to surprise you with new thoughts, experiences, and adventure. He is ever ready to tell you secrets and mysteries about plans for you and His kingdom. He has thoughts to share with just you! Can you imagine how special He thinks you are? The Beloved is perfect in the way He loves and always attentive to your heart, thoughts, desires, and needs.

Notice too how reassuring Beloved is about the Shulamite's identity by calling her "fair one, my love." The identity of the Shulamite is representative of women and men. The Beloved describes the Shulamite as beautiful without spot or blemish when He calls her the "fair one." When you consider the Shulamite as representative of a man as well, then he would be considered handsome without spot or blemish in the eyes of the Beloved. The beauty the Beloved sees is not only the outward flesh, but inward core of a man or woman's heart. No matter what they have done in their life to cause them to feel shame, guilt or anything considered wayward, the Beloved sees them with a perspective of hope and restoration. Whether you are male or female, if you set your gaze upon the Beloved, His reflection will begin to be seen in you. This is because a love that is perfect knows perfectly all about the object of their affection, you.

Consider this story for a moment. This story is about a young man who grew up fatherless with little hope for his future. This story could even be of a young man that has a father, but the father is not emotionally present and not encouraging in this young man's life. In despair and desperation to seek comfort, solace, and some kind of understanding about who he is and where he is going, he makes choices that lead him on a very difficult journey. He desperately wants encouragement and identity; a sense of belonging and confidence. He wants someone to believe in him enough to know he can do great things in his life. He encounters a very wise and gentle man one day along his journey. This man speaks to him about a destiny and purpose the young man dared not ever dream because of lack of confidence and despair. The young man was so drawn to the wise man that he followed him everywhere even though he had very little strength to do so. The young man observed his every reaction to situations and how the wise man was so full of compassion and love for every soul he met. The wise man would spend hours and hours with the young man speaking to him of dreams and a future he could see for him. You see, the wise man knew all things and could see past the crippling choices the young man had made. The wise man knew all the wrong choices the young man made could be turned into good if only the young would believe it and continue to learn from him. The young man began to look just like the wise man; he began to take on his character and soon the pain of his past and all the choices he had made that took him down the wrong paths began to be turned into compassion for others as the wise man taught him how to use the horrible things of his past to bring healing to those he encountered along his journey. The young man whose head was held low as he walked and only confusion and despair engulfed his soul began to be confident in who he was created to be. He began to look upward because he knew the wise man loved him and would always reassure him of his destiny because the wise man loved him with a perfect love. Because of the wise man, the young man began to understand that he is more than choices he has made or his past mistakes, or the problems he has created. The wise man gently remade him into a man of courage and compassion as the young man walked side by side the wise man watching his every move.

Imagine a similar story about a young woman. She finds herself all alone sitting in the corner of a crowded room, invited by people who she considers surface friends. The room is filled with people but she feels alone as her mind is consumed with glimpses of choices she has made. Her feelings tell her everyone can see what she has done and the shame that clouds her mind. The shame hovers over her like darkness. The shame turns into fear of reaching out to those around. She desperately wants to be loved but the emotional pain of her choices weighs her down and she has become too weak to hope. A man walks into the crowded room and she senses something gentle and genuine about him. He comes toward her as if his entire reason for being there was to search her out. Their eyes catch one another as he continues to walk closer to where she sits in the corner. Her attention goes to him and everyone else in the room seems to fade in her mind. He stops and stands directly in front of her. She notices his eyes are filled with compassion she has never seen before. He begins to tell her there is a message he has come to deliver. The message is from someone greater than even he. He begins to recite from his heart the message and says, "You have made choices that have caused you pain and those are mistakes that haunt your soul. You have let those mistakes define who you are and shame grips your soul. You are weak and feel hopeless to ever try again but I know you desperately want to be loved. You are not who you think you are. You are far more than the choices you have made and there is a love that awaits you if only you believe. Even though you are weak, just believe and love will do the rest. Love will remake you and take away the shame, fear and hopelessness of the past. A love like mine can do this because I fought for you and won; I paid your debts of all your mistakes so that your identity could be secure. My name is Perfect Love and I've come to restore your soul." Tears filled her eyes and for the first time she could see herself from Perfect Love's eyes. The shame was washed away in a moment as she began to believe and trust a love that had the power to change her and heal her soul.

These stories could be of anyone and the facts or circumstances can look several different ways yet yield the same feelings of despair. Truth is, He continually reaffirms our identity over and over and over again. No matter what we have done, no matter what we think of ourselves, and no matter what others may think of us, His opinion is the only one that matters. The Beloved knows the importance of infusing your soul with His perspective and thoughts concerning you. Infusion of these thoughts concerning your identity is vital to your life being full and complete, living above the old tapes that have played over and over in your mind, living as though your soul is infused with heaven's nature. Christ is heaven's perfect One, and His glory is what He wants to impart to you. You becoming like Christ, fashioned in the special design He created when He formed your personality and being. This, the Beloved's pursuit of you, is His purpose and goal. Christ's death was a high price to pay, therefore He will allow nothing to stop Him from accomplishing His purpose. The price Christ paid was so you could understand and reflect His compelling love and nature. As you gaze upon Christ (the Beloved), His very nature is transferred in you. Christ is perfect and relentless in His pursuit of your heart. He will find you at every turn. You cannot run away from Perfect Love.

Stop for a brief moment and think about those people in your life who encouraged you when times were difficult and where every place you looked seemed to be a "winter in your soul." The old saying, "When it rains, it two pours," is so true at times. We have all felt the dark nights of the soul in our lives. In chapter two, the Beloved is declaring and proclaiming that the dark winter season of your life is over. He declares that the "springtime has come" and newness of life and love is available.

A turtledove is heard in the land—meaning, the call of life, abundance, and love want to find a solid place in you, but will you accept? Are you a visionary for your life? Can you see what the Beloved sees even if it is a small fragment of the vision? Proverbs 29:18 says, "My people perish for lack of vision." Confusion, despair and hopelessness will set into our souls when we do not have a vision, dream or purpose to focus our attention. But it cannot be just any dream, vision or purpose. It must be the purpose you were created to fulfill. Any purpose or vision that you attempt to fulfill that is not fashioned for you will feel unsettling in your soul. The right vision supplies your soul with a peace and contentment knowing you are doing what you were created to do and be who you were created to be. The Beloved knows your purpose and unfolds how He sees you at the same time. He is encouraging the Shulamite to move forward and looking toward what lies ahead when He said that the fruit of the fig tree is abundant and new growth from the grapes is springing forth. Your life is like the fig tree and the new growth seen on the grape vine. Many of you reading are saying, "But it certainly does not look like it because I'm still in the 'when it rains, it pours' place." That is a reality here on earth, but there is another heavenly reality that is just as real—in fact, even more real. It is the perspective and vision for your life that the Beloved wants to show you. The Beloved is calling you to a secret place in the cleft of the rocks where only He can see you and you can only hear His voice. He wants His word to wash over you and your soul to become still and quiet. He wants your thoughts to be of Him only as you draw away with Him. When you go to this special place, the cries of His lovesick heart over you is felt and heard. The turtledove represents the voice of Perfect Love calling you to a life that is full and a love that brings hope. Will you respond? Even though the present circumstances look to be horrible, there is hope. And even if the complete purpose and value for your life is still unclear, you have decided to put one foot in front of the other and hide yourself away with Him. In this secret place you will be found, and new life will spring forth. The winter fades, and the springtime begins as you decide to move toward Perfect Love.

> ***Prayer:*** Dear Beloved, I desire to be aligned with your perfect vision and purpose for my life. Too long I have seen myself in a distorted way and not from your Perfect Love. I desire to see myself from your perspective. Remove the veils that keep me from more clear vision of who I am and what I was created to do. Show me those things I must let go of that have side tracked my identity, purpose, and vision. I am willing to let them go. I know that all my mistakes and choices of the past can and will be used for the good of my future because you are a God of restoration and mercy. Heavenly Father, above all else let me feel and know your love for me every step of the way. I will not and cannot go this path alone. In Jesus's name, Amen.

At the Core of His Heart

> Set me as a seal upon your heart, as a seal upon your arm; for love is as strong as death, jealousy as cruel as the grave. Its flames are flames of fire, a most vehement flame. Many waters cannot quench love, nor can the floods drown it. If a man would give for love all the wealth of his house, it would be utterly despised.
>
> —Song of Solomon 8:6–7

In the Song of Solomon, the Shulamite expresses a deep committed love to the Beloved by asking to be a "seal upon His heart and upon His arm." A seal represents a signature and authority, and it makes a profound statement when the seal is put upon the heart of someone very special. A heart beats to the rhythm of life in it; a heart feels deeply and pulses the cleansing attribute of life itself through the blood that flows through it. The heart is the core of a man. She wants to give herself away to Him. She wants to dwell in the inner most part of the Beloved where life flows, and she is at the center of the cleansing power of the blood that flows through His heart because she is the seal. How profound. She is saying, "Let me be at the center of all you want to do and everywhere you go. Take me with you. Don't ever forget me. Let me be a part of your plans, dreams, and aspirations." She knows she belongs nowhere else but at the core of His heart. Beat by beat, moment by moment, she feels the intensity of what He wants and what His plans are because she is at the center of His heart, hearing every heartbeat. She is a garden enclosed, a seal upon His heart. Her life has no meaning without Him. If she cannot be the seal upon His heart, life is useless because love flows from this heart. Their love is a "vehement flame." The value of this love cannot, nor ever will, be measured by any standard on this earth except the price that the Beloved was willing to pay to secure the love of His Shulamite. That price is the fuel that makes this kind of love a "vehement flame." Oh, to be loved with a flame that never quenches and never ceases. To be adored with eyes that burn with passion and fire for the one who is at the center of this unquenched and unselfish love.

Not only does she want to be the seal upon his heart, but she wants to be the seal upon his arm as well. The descriptive words that connote *arm* include might, power, strength, help, savior, deliver, protection, ruling, power. She is telling her beloved that she wants to do the things he can do. She wants to collaborate with him in His purpose. She wants her purpose to be the same as His. As we walk through this life, God wants us to realize more and more our purpose. Our first purpose for creation was to "worship Him in spirit and truth." He created a people He could have fellowship with, and we were formed in His likeness. I believe the delight that God feels in His heart when we worship Him with our work, our praise, our finances, resources, and even in the stillness of waiting is unfathomable. His heart is moved far more with emotion than ours. We can feel a touch of this delight if we get still enough and take the time to be with Him and Him alone. He draws us to this place of being with Him. He woos us over and over and over again. He never gives up. His compelling love and devotion for us is the strength that continues to draw close to us. In unity, we establish together what His "arm" does on earth. We become His strength, His mouthpiece, His righteous vessels of honor and His authority, and we wield the sword with the strength of that arm. The sword is part of the armor He gives us, which is the Word of God. Our arm is strong to wield the sword because we recognize the purpose for our very being and the likeness between Him and us. The likeness has manifested itself out of deep, devoted love, the bonds of which cannot easily be broken—forever being pursued, adored, and loved with an abandoned love that conquers all fear and unbelief. He is our prize, and we are His special ones.

Relentless Love

Imagine for a moment the Lord's perfect heart and you, His special one, at the center. You are nestled right at the center where the blood comes in and flows out. As the blood comes into His heart, it completely washes over you. You are so attached and nestled that as the warmth of His blood flows over you with each heartbeat, you are cleansed and refreshed. His heartbeat for you is relentless; it does exactly what it was designed to do—wash you, protect you, hold you, renew you, and keep you at His center. If you tried to leave the center of this perfect heart where love flows, He would know you were missing, and you would feel lost. The effect on Him would be an ache that would compel Him to come after you. You would feel completely lost apart from Him, and the cleansing and renewing you always felt would no longer be felt. But this separation propels Him to come after you because He knows the safest and most secure place for you in this world is at the core of His heart. The love He has for you is so strong and He will allow nothing to separate you from Him except your own will to remove yourself. Even then, His love is relentless and will seek after you.

> Awake, O north wind, and come, O south! Blow upon my garden, that its spices may flow out. Let my

beloved come to his garden and eat its pleasant fruits.

—Song of Solomon 4:16

A garden enclosed is my sister, my spouse, a spring shut up, a fountain sealed.

—Song of Solomon 4:12

The journey of your life is weaved carefully and lovingly by Him, and He will never let you go. His love is so relentless that even in times that you are unfaithful, He will seek you and find you at every turn. The journey of your life has been destined by Him. Each of us has a destiny that leads closer to His purpose. There is no other thing, lover, or friend that cares more about you than the Beloved. This relentless, perfect love is ever pursuing and exciting. You will have valleys and mountains to climb, but He will be in the lowest low and on the mountaintop.

In the valleys, your heart and true character will be tested and formed. The north winds are those testings, trials, and tribulations that come to us in this fallen world, whether by the hand of the enemy of our soul, others, or ourselves. The north winds blow upon your life so that the fragrance of Him will be ever present, dripping from your heart. There is no other way, beloved. The nature of man is such that unless enough pressure is applied, change does not typically occur. Some heed wise counsel and sound advice, but most learn life lessons the hard way. The north winds will blow upon your life, exerting the pressure you need through suffering and difficulty that will transform you into a radiant creature to carry His glory and presence if you will allow the transformation. It is not pleasant at the time and certainly does not feel good, but you will be morphed into being more like Him. He is the potter and you are the clay. He is the sculptor and you are the piece of art to be chiseled. Pressure from being molded and chiseled will at times feel unbearable, but you will survive because His love knows just how much pressure to apply making a strong warrior and beautiful bride, fashioned for the King. He will then come with the south wind and blow upon your life pleasure and blessing. Relief is there and will come. Sometimes the north and south winds blow simultaneously and we know not when they will come.

Consider the majesty of an eagle for a moment. Eagles are strong and they soar with grace. They can spot their prey from a long distance, for their vision is clear. They can see things from a perspective many creatures can never see. When an eagle becomes ill, it plants itself at the highest place it can find and lays on its back, allowing the sun to purge its body completely until all the feathers have fallen off. As uncomfortable and vulnerable as the eagle is while the transformation and purging is taking place, it knows this is the only way to have complete healing and strength to continue its purpose. This behavior is both natural and uncomfortable. In many ways, we are like a majestic eagle, and the purging and cleansing of our life is sometimes painful and uncomfortable. We know when we have been met with a north wind that has come to purify. At the end of the purging and healing process, the eagle experiences more grace and strength than before. New feathers grow back and transformation has taken place. This is the season of being refreshed for the eagle. The south wind comes and connects perfectly with his wings, propelling him to soar stronger and freer than before. This uncomfortable process is because of the Beloved's relentless love for us. He knows us better than we know ourselves and which wind to allow.

If you have ever experienced true love, then you have had a glimpse of relentless love. There is *nothing* a man will not do for the woman he loves. If she is hurting, he will comfort her no matter what his need or condition. If she is in danger, he will die for her, taking no thought of his own life. If she is in need, he will find a way to give what she needs. True, abiding, relentless love has multiple aspects of expression. Relentless love speaks in infinite ways and contains varied descriptions. We can find the beauty of this kind of love between a man and a woman which is wonderful. But even more satisfying is when we experience this kind of love between our Lord and His first love—you.

One day as I was sitting at a coffee shop studying the Song of Solomon, the Lord spoke to my heart clearly that if a woman will set her gaze upon Jesus and His character, and allow Him to love her, she will be fashioned into a beautiful bride with much grace and beauty. Then, after a season she will be prepared to meet the true man He has for her. She will recognize him. So I said to the Lord I understand, but what about the man? The thought came to mind a man must do the same. He must set his gaze upon Jesus which will fashion him into a warrior and gentleman. Christ will bring that beautiful woman into his life, but not until his character has been formed more into Christ's image.

Oh! The mistake we make often is getting ahead of God and trying to force a relationship to work or look for someone to fill the void in our soul! We see that *waiting* is difficult and we try to birth an Ishmael. God will bless our Ishmaels, but Isaacs are His first choice. Bringing this special companion into our life is in God's perfect timing and this special companion will be used in our life to help shape and form us into more of His image. This does mean there is truly a preparation period of time and waiting before the timing is right. One of the main reasons God puts a man and woman together is to form their character more to His image, using their union to bring this transformation. Timing is everything.

God promises to take the dry desert places of our lives and turn them into refreshing springs of water for our soul. Isaiah 41:17–18 promises this refreshing: "The poor and needy seek water, but there is none, their tongues fail for thirst. I, the Lord, will hear them; I, the God of Israel, will not forsake them. I will open rivers in desolate heights, and fountains in the midst of the valleys; I will make the wilderness a pool of water, and the dry land springs of water." The desert places of our lives need to be watered near the refreshing springs, rivers, and fountains that flow. Uncontaminated and pure reservoirs are where we feed and grow. The Shulamite understood this when she inquired to her Beloved (Song of Solomon 1:7–10), "Tell me, O you whom I love, where you feed your flock, where you make it rest at noon. For why should I be as one who veils herself by the flocks of your Companion?" And He answers, "If you do not know, O fairest among women, follow in the footsteps of the flock, and feed Your little goats beside the shepherds tents. I have compared you, my love, to my filly among Pharaoh's chariots. Your cheeks are lovely with ornaments, your neck with chains of gold."

The Shulamite refers to herself as being veiled. She does not feel or think she is like the flock. She looks at herself as being "different" from the rest of the flock. The veil she wears is woven to look like the culture of the world and the agenda of the world. The Beloved agrees with her, but not in the way she would expect! He sees her "fairest" and the "filly" among Pharaoh's chariots. The Beloved's comment and definition of the Shulamite is lavish, truthful, and extreme. She is not seeing in herself what He is seeing, but He compels her to come closer among the "shepherds' tents" so that she begins to unveil herself and see what He sees in her as she feeds, grows, and rests among the companions. He wants her to bring her goats, those whom He has given her to protect, mentor, and serve. He beckons her to bring her world into His world and those whom she loves. He wants her to be nestled at the "core of His heart." There is a power that is greater and force that is stronger than our sinful nature. It is *God's desire for us*. If God is for me, who could be against me? You can run or hide, but you are seen and known. The lover of your soul will find you again and again… and yet again.

> *Prayer:* Beloved, I'm beginning to understand that I need to be nestled at the core of your heart where your cleansing blood can flow over me. I'm also beginning to realize that if I leave this place I will feel lost eventually. Help me to remain at the center of your heart for this is a place of safety. This is where your love flows and my healing is complete. I see your love is perfect, relentless, and calling out to me. I give you permission now to save me from myself and my circumstances and capture my heart fully so I will know

who I am, why I was created and how much I am loved. In Jesus's name, Amen.

WHO ARE YOU?

It's Monday morning. As I sit to spend time with the Lord, I listen to a song by Sarah Edwards at the International House of Prayer. It says, "We are still His beautiful rose that He takes such delight in even when our own hearts condemn us." Please ponder that statement a few minutes. Read it over and over until you get a glimpse of what God is saying to us. The depth of His love is unfathomable at times. How can you explain a love of that depth? Is it even possible? Writing now, I'm at a loss for words to describe this love. How many times has your heart told you how horrible you are, how you will never reach the goal, how others are so much better than you, how shameful and degrading your choices have been, and how hopeless your situation is because of you? Beloved, you are beautiful to Him even in all your weakness. He delights in you, always. Your heart is not able to love you like He does. No one person has the right to define who you are, not even yourself, except God. Your heart does not see what He sees in you. He wants your heart to see from His eyes. When the veil that keeps you from seeing yourself from the loving eyes of this magnificently perfect Heavenly Father is removed then you realize you are truly His beloved and He loves the things you do, think, say. He loves your thoughts and knows where you're going. This is His delight and joy—to look at you and see how beautiful you are as you respond to His love.

Many songs, poems, and stories have been written about God's great love. God's love is measureless, enduring eternally, pure and full of wonderful surprises. Words cannot describe Perfect Love justly and experiencing this kind of pure love leaves you speechless when your soul is encountered by it. Beloved, He is a faithful witness, and everything He says and does is true. Every word He says about you is true.

The problem is we do not know what He is saying about us. I have asked many people, "What do you think God says about you and what does He think about you?" Most cannot answer the question because they truly do not know. The Song of Solomon is one of the most beautiful books of the Bible that describes His thoughts toward His Bride. Knowing who you are and how He sees you is a process. Some of us receive extremely clear understanding early in life as to how the Heavenly Father sees us. A clear understanding early in life of the Heavenly Father's perspective is most likely because of such healthy relationships with our earthly father and mother. We live today in a fatherless generation. As a result, we have people, even believers, walking around feeling like an orphan, not feeling loved, not loving themselves, and not knowing who they are or why they were created.

I Am a Lily

> Like a lily among thorns, so is my love among the daughters.
>
> —Song of Solomon 2:2

> Where has your Beloved gone, O fairest among women? Where has your Beloved turned aside that we may seek him with you? My beloved has gone to his garden to the beds of spices, *to feed his flock in the gardens, and to gather lilies.* I am my Beloved's, and my beloved is mine. *He feeds his flock among the lilies.*
>
> —Song of Solomon 6:1–3; italics mine

> "The lilies of the field are the scarlet poppies which bloom from a bulb after the spring rains. Lilies bloom for only one day and carpet the plains and hills of Palestine with colorful blossoms. In their brief life, they are clothed with a beauty which surpasses the beauty of the robes of kings."
>
> —quote from David Padfield,
> the Church of Christ in Zion, Illinois

In the Song of Solomon 2:2, the Beloved recognizes the Shulamite's dedication to Him calling her a lily. The lily is special and majestic, unlike the thorns that may surround them. The thorns in the Shulamite's life represent others who have not yet given their hearts over to a place of adoration and focus on the Beloved. They are in need of the Beloved's touch. The Beloved sees the purity of the Shulamite's heart toward Him compared to others. In the Song of Solomon 6:1–3, the Shulamite knows the way for her heart to remain steadfast with a consistent gaze upon Him is to dwell among other lilies with hearts much like her own--a love for the Beloved. The garden represents the life of the Shulamite, and in this garden the Beloved will dwell, continually revealing her identity and abundantly meeting her needs spiritually, emotionally and physically. The Shulamite knows how special she is to the Beloved and how special the other lilies are too!

How special do you truly feel? If you look deep within, can you answer this question with complete honesty? I believe the majority of people do not feel or believe they are that special to God or to people. They don't even feel very special to themselves. But I believe they completely want to believe how special they are to God and others. They not only want to believe it, but they want to feel it. This book is written from the depths of my own heart's cry—a compelling desire to know how special I am to God. A realization must occur in your heart. Many of us have a head knowledge of being special to God but have never experienced the unfailing specialness of His love from their hearts. It truly can be not only knowledge but a sincere, true feeling that stands the test of time.

A true feeling of God's love is not gained because you perform correctly and do everything right. It does not come to you because your "list" has been checked off of what you have accomplished. It comes because He has such a love for you all the time that no matter what you do, good or bad, right or wrong, perfect or imperfect nothing can change how special you are to Him and His love for you. Stop and think about how special you are for a moment. You are so special that He was willing to painfully die on a cross, being stripped of everything while standing bare and open to His onlookers, knowing the price He was paying took care of your healing emotionally and physically once and for all time and set in motion the plan for you to rule and reign with Him eternally. It's because He wanted to be with you and cherish you and adore you for all eternity on earth and in heaven. It's because you are so special and His desire for you is unquenchable.

Ponder on this statement: no one has the right to define who you are but God! But if we are honest, we have allowed others or our own limited thinking to determine who we are, how we see ourselves, and how special we feel about ourselves, which in turn has distorted a healthy perspective of how God sees us and how special we truly are to Him.

His amazing grace is something we need to learn about for a lifetime. His amazing grace is *love's compelling power to uphold you in the darkest moments of your life; it is this power of grace that gives you strength to overcome and provides you cleansing and healing when you fail to allow grace to uphold you in righteousness.* I use to think grace was only His kindness and mercy toward me when I failed to follow him or sinned. Now I realize more than ever that it is His compelling love and strength for each and every moment we face in this life. It is His truth that stands the test. The Heavenly Father understands your weaknesses and has provided strength through His grace to overcome. He looks at your desire to rely upon this strength called grace. Your desire comes from your heart. This is what He sees and what He calls beautiful and fair. Just like the lily of the fields, so are you--loved because of who you were created to be, not because of what you have or have not done. The Shulamite understands how special she is to the Beloved and the importance of remaining close to Him. She realizes her strength is found where He dwells, and among the other lilies, not among the thorns.

You Are My Fairest One

The Shulamite begins to come into agreement with the Beloved's identity of her. She has continued gazing on the Beloved and her transformation is taking place. Being loved perfectly makes us feel special and like we are the favorite one! The relationship between the Beloved and the Shulamite is much like a dance. Step by step, each one's awareness of the other's move is anticipated. The Shulamite knows her best effort to flow gracefully comes when she completely trust the leadership of the Beloved as they dance. The rhythm of the dance becomes perfectly synchronized when her gaze is completely upon Him. She could close her eyes and follow perfectly because she has observed, sensed, learned, and practiced the steps of the Beloved.

"You Are My Fairest One" discloses our identity as we can see from the Scriptures that follow. Think of the following Scriptures' descriptions like each different rhythmic move from the dance between the Beloved and Shulamite. Each Scripture has its own expression just like each move of their dance. The Beloved describes us with words spoken through Scriptures in chapter four of the Song of Solomon.

> Behold, you are fair, my love! Behold, you are fair? You have dove's eyes behind your veil. Your hair is like a flock of goats, going down from Mount Gilead.
>
> —Song of Solomon 4:1

He calls her "fair," meaning, she is beautiful to look at and gaze upon. But she is fair in her heart toward Him. The outward beauty is not what He is focused on, but it is her heart's desire to know Him more. He calls her His love. There is no other love. She is the special one, close to His heart. She has dove's eyes—meaning, He notices that her gaze is for Him and Him alone; she is focused. Her eyes are steadfast on the object of her affection and nothing else has her attention. She is covered and adorned with His glory as her hair is described flowing down from Mount Gilead.

> Your teeth are like a flock of shorn sheep which have come up from the washing. Every one of which bears twins, and none is barren among them. Your lips are like a strand of scarlet, and your mouth is lovely. Your temples behind your veil are like a piece of pomegranate.
>
> —Song of Solomon 4:2–3

He pays attention to every detail about you. When your life depends on His word and what He thinks, you are washed, and He becomes the bread of life that you chew on. There is no barrenness to your life but fruitfulness and multiplication when you make His word your life-giving substance. When you speak, you do so with wisdom and grace. Your temples are a place where your emotions and thoughts are seated. He describes your temples like a "piece of pomegranate." A pomegranate is a fruit that is very high in antioxidants. At the very core of the pomegranate, there is white pulp, and the juice from this fruit is red. The symbol of a pomegranate was also worn on the robe of the priests. It represents the purity of Christ and the blood He shed so you could be covered in holiness and purity forever. Your temples (emotions) are lovely to Him as He knows all your thoughts toward Him. Your emotions and thoughts toward Him moves His heart.

Song of Solomon 4:4 says, "Your neck is like the tower of David, built for an armory, on which hang a thousand bucklers." You can walk in honor and authority because you were made to see from a high place where to go and what the plans of the enemy may be. You have shields (bucklers) and weapons of warfare, which have been granted to you because of the authority you walk with. You are honored and revered because He gives you this honor and authority. You carry Him in your heart wherever you go. When David faced Goliath, he attempted first to wear the armor of Saul. Saul's armor did not fit David. David's armor was crafted in the depths of his heart in the wilderness being alone with God. He knew His authority when he faced Goliath. He could approach Goliath with strong resolve and belief that he would defeat his enemy. He looked up with strength and used the wisdom of God to defeat a giant. The same is true for you. Do you see yourself with this kind of strength and authority, or do you shrink back? The honor He has bestowed upon you has nothing to do with what you have done to gain it. It has everything to do with Perfect Love. He defeated death, hell, and the grave at His death and resurrection so that He could bestow upon you His authority and strength to face your enemy. The problem most of us experience is we do not know and believe that we carry

His authority. His death's meaning would be futile and of no avail if He was not able to give us His character and authority. That was His purpose, and He wants us to believe the strength He has given to us freely.

> Your two breasts are like two fawns, twins of a gazelle, which feed among the lilies.
>
> —Song of Solomon 4:5

Your life is fruitful, and you wear the breastplate of righteousness. You are among others that know where to get strength and restoration (among the lilies). You gather together and encourage each other. Even though each one of you is different, you have the Beloved that watches over each of you and cares for your needs. There is no place for self-sufficiency in His love. Your identity is continually revealed as you gaze on Him. As you make His plans for your life your plans, you grow in fruitfulness and likeness of Him and He promises emotional, physical and spiritual provision for you, always. As you grow in trust of His love, it becomes apparent to others around you that there is a solid peace that covers you. You become more like Him in that you want others to feel what you feel and see what you see. Life has new meaning because of Perfect Love. You are compelled to share what you have found with others for their encouragement and identity. You become more aware they desire and need what you have been given.

Song of Solomon 4:6 says, "Until the day breaks and the shadows flee away, I will go my way to the mountain of myrrh and to the hill of frankincense." The Beloved is telling His beloved that He will suffer for her, looking forward to the shadow of the suffering to pass. His love for her is so sure and perfect, He will gladly pay the price for her destiny. Because of the price He is willing to pay for her life and destiny, He can then say what He sees as described in the verse that follows: "You are fair, my love, and there is no spot in you" (Song of Solomon 4:7). Why? Because Love has covered her and died for her, and Love's own identity and destiny has been given to her. When He looks upon her, He sees a reflection of Himself. He was intentional in His pain and suffering. He knew what it would cost Him to bestow upon her authority, value, and destiny, and He willingly gave Himself because He is Perfect Love. It is finished and done forever. There is nothing left for the beloved to do but worship, love, and adore Him. This she gladly does because Love has compelled her and drawn her. They are beginning to become one, and the dance of love begins. Abiding with each other is all that matters, and life takes on a new meaning.

> Come with me from Lebanon, my spouse; with me from Lebanon. Look from the top of Amana, from

> the top of Senir and Hermon, from the lion's dens, from the mountains of the leopards.
>
> —Song of Solomon 4:8

The lions' dens and mountains of the leopards are symbolic of the enemy of our soul. He is the father of lies, and because of the position we hold with our Beloved, he hates us. His every move is to strike and devour, sidetrack, and defeat. If he can destroy or harm you, then he feels he has accomplished harm to the Lord. The leopard is likened to a swift enemy or foe against the beloved. In Revelation 13:2, the leopard represents an Antichrist enraged against mankind. These two beasts linger in the borders of Lebanon mountain area. This mountainous area represent a place where danger lurks. In this verse, the Beloved is asking his fairest one to look beyond this area into a place of safety and to come away from this place of danger. He calls his beloved to safety and warns her of lingering in a place of danger. This place of danger is where compromise can take root. This is a place where a heart unsettled and unstable in the direction the Beloved has for her can find devastation of the soul. He explains that staying in this place is not where she belongs, and her identity is not found here, but destroyed. He is determined to lead the beloved to safety, and she needs only to listen and follow. He calls and calls until she looks His direction, and then His heart is overcome, and He knows He has the beloved's attention.

> Thou has ravished my heart, My sister, bride; thou has ravished My heart with one look from thine eyes, with one chain of thy neck.
>
> —Song of Solomon 4:9

Can you remember a time when you were in the same room with someone whom you knew adored you? If you have experienced this kind of adoration, then you will understand better what one look from the Beloved toward us does to our emotions. When you are adored and you know the one who adores you is staring at you with eyes of peace, compassion, and desire to express their intense love for you, it moves your soul in ways that only those who have been loved can fully understand. What is the feeling you have when you catch a glimpse of this moment? It's a feeling that you are the most beautiful and special person in the eyes of your beholder at that very moment. When love is there, you don't care who sees the two of you looking at one another. The entire world and others around you are at a distance when there is just the two of you caught in a moment of full attention, looking into each other's eyes.

What does a ravished heart feel like, and what are the actions of a person whose heart is ravished by the one that fully catches their attention? The word "ravish" is described as being carried away with deep emotion toward something; to be enraptured; to overwhelm with emotion; to give great delight to. The intense power of your glance towards the

Beloved moves His heart with great emotion. In His eyes you are everything. His heart is ravished and you are seen as the most beautiful creature without spot or blemish. You are more beautiful than the angels! He also feels your adoration for Him as you exchange a glance. His ravished heart compels Him to listen to what you have to say. You are becoming convinced that He will protect and love you. You can fully trust Him. He is so ravished by your glance that He calls you "His sister, His bride." Whether you are male or female, the symbolism is the same. You are a special creature who can move the heart of God to a place of intense emotion. The Beloved is the author of emotion and He created you to have a ravished heart for Him as He does for you. When your emotions are intense in love toward Him, you *always* have His attention. This is who you are; a lover of God who can move the heart of Him that created you.

Your neck represents your authority. A beautiful chain or piece of jewelry around your neck represents honor and glory, much like the reason a queen will wear her most precious jewels around her neck when she is to be seen. She carries a beauty, grace, and glory that is only given to her. The same is true for you as the beloved that is adored. You are given authority, and the choices you make are important to the one who loves you. When you choose to use the honor and authority that is bestowed upon you to look in His direction, He knows you are faithful, and He is the only one who has your full attention. You can walk in assurance of strength and authority knowing that when you glance His way with full attention, there is nothing He will not do for you. You are loved beyond measure. This is who you are.

> How fair is your love my sister, my spouse. How much better than wine is your love, and the scent of perfumes than all spices!
>
> —Song of Solomon 4:10

He begins to explain what your love is like to Him after you look His way. He is convinced of your love, and your love for Him is described as fair—meaning pure, undefiled, true, attentive, compassionate, and focused. Wine represents all the pleasures and riches the world has to offer. He describes your love as better than all the riches the world has to offer. No spice exists that is more fragrant and special than the scent of your compelling and adoring love for Him. Your love for Him exudes a scented perfume representing your life. You are covered with His fragrance and are beginning to smell like Him. Your life gives off a fragrance everywhere you go. Mary anointed Him for His burial with all that she had left of her inheritance. This very act was a pouring out of her life and was a fragrance that filled the room. Your life fills the rooms every place you go, and your love fills His heart with intense love and emotion at every glance toward Him. You can change the atmosphere in places when your life is a perfumed scent representing the Beloved's love.

> Your lips, oh my spouse, drip as the honeycomb. Honey and milk are under your tongue; and the fragrance of your garments is like the fragrance of Lebanon.
>
> —Song of Solomon 4:11

What kind of words do you speak about others, Christ, and yourself? Is your conversation seasoned with kindness, gentleness, encouragement, wisdom, and truth? The power of the tongue is sometimes underestimated. James 3:5–11 says:

> Even so the tongue is a little member and boasts great things. See how great a forest a little fire kindles! And the tongue is a fire, a world of iniquity. The tongue is so set among our members that it defiles the whole body, and sets on fire the course of nature; and it is set on fire by hell. For every kind of beast and bird, of reptile and creature of the sea, is tamed and has been tamed by mankind. But no man can tame the tongue. It is an unruly evil, full of deadly poison. With it we bless our God and Father, and with it we curse men, who have been made in the similitude of God. Out of the same mouth proceed blessing and cursing. My brethren, these things ought not to be so. Does a spring send forth fresh water and bitter from the same opening?

Clearly, the tongue is untamable and unruly without a heart full of what the Beloved says. He is truth. Proverbs 16:24 says, "Pleasant words are like a honeycomb, sweetness to the soul and health to the bones." When the written and living Word is deeply embedded in our hearts, there is a transformation that takes place, and bitter, devastating words are replaced with pure truth. Psalm 19:10 describes the Word of God as "more to be desired are they than gold, yea, than much fine gold; sweeter also than honey and the honeycomb."

In Proverbs 16:23 we are told that "the heart of the wise instructs his mouth and adds learning to his lips." We have the ability to change our thoughts and our conversation by allowing the Word of God and truth to become our foundation and filter. When the children of Israel were told they would enter the promised land, honey and milk were some of the promised blessings they would encounter. Milk and honey are symbolic of abundance and nourishment. They both represent spiritual blessings and edification. When we speak words that edify, encourage, and exhort, we release spiritual blessings. What we say matters, and the Beloved sees the one He loves has gotten to a place where her speech is seasoned with wisdom. What she says about Him, others, and themselves brings life. He recognizes the transformation that has taken place in her heart where she has allowed His thoughts and character to permeate her words. He is affirming her in what He sees and hears from her conversation.

> A garden enclosed is my sister, my spouse, a spring shut up, a fountain sealed. Your plants are an orchard of pomegranates with pleasant fruits, fragrant henna with spikenard, spikenard and saffron, calamus and cinnamon, with all trees of frankincense, myrrh and aloes, with all the chief spices—a fountain of gardens, a well of living waters, and streams from Lebanon.
>
> —Song of Solomon 4:12–15

The Beloved represents the actions and thoughts of our Lord Jesus Christ. There are two gardens in which he passes through. One is the garden of Gethsemane, where he agonized for hours, sweating blood because of what he was about to face on the cross. His struggle was unimaginably intense because of the suffering he was about to experience so that His beloved could live, reign, and rule with Him in eternity. The next garden was the garden where he was placed inside a tomb, which was sealed by a stone.

You are His beloved, and you will go through the garden of suffering in your life, agonizing over betrayals and losses, grief and unpleasant experiences just as your Beloved did in the garden of Gethsemane as He prepared His heart to take on the sin of the world. Through your suffering you will identify with the Beloved. This is not because He desires for you to suffer, but it is a result of sin in the world. He promises to turn all your "ashes into beauty" because He paid the price for you. You will pass through the garden in the tomb as you allow the Beloved's love and character be resurrected in you. You will decrease as He increases in your life; you will reflect Him more and more. You are His beloved and His garden enclosed. You are His closest companion whom He calls His sister and His spouse because He can trust you to allow His likeness be formed in you. The Beloved, being Jesus Christ, is the spring shut up, the fountain sealed as portrayed by the stone covering the tomb. He was sealed in the tomb until He rose on the third day. He came forth as a spring of living water. Your life is sealed in Him when you realize you are His beloved.

When your life reflects the Beloved, you are an enclosed garden reflecting heaven on earth. Your life is the garden, and out of it flows pleasant fragrance and fruit just as it did from His life. In your garden is an orchard of many pleasant fruits. What you do, what you think, and how you love determines the quality of your garden. The pomegranate is symbolic of fruitfulness. The design of the pomegranate dangled as trim on the ends of the priest's ephod. The pomegranate has always been symbolic of fruitfulness because it represents Christ's suffering and resurrection. The pomegranate's red juice represents His blood that was shed for you, and the pulp of the fruit is white, depicting

His holiness. The fruitfulness of your life has value when you are hidden in Him because He paved the way by giving Himself for you. We are His fruits here on earth.

Spikenard is a rare and costly fragrant oil made from a flowering plant of Valerian family, and it is also called nard. It is used as perfume and incense and is considered a luxury. It was offered as incense on the altar in the tabernacle. It fills the room with a distinct, pleasant aroma.

Spikenard was used by Mary of Bethany to anoint Jesus head and feet before His burial. Her act was one of total abandonment. This very act of love for her Beloved told Him that He was more costly and precious to her than anything else in her world; this oil was her life savings, and she loved Him enough to pour all that she had left upon Him. She wanted the world to know His love and sacrifice leaves an impressionable fragrance worth all riches and more. When we are found in Him, our life exudes the same fragrance because of love.

Spikenard is also called "fragrance of the bride" depicting a bride who has made herself ready to be married. You, as His beloved, are being prepared for that day when you will join Him completely in eternity.

The Beloved also describes her as "spikenard and saffron." Spikenard, being the costly, rare perfume and incense, is mixed with saffron, which is one of world's most costly spices. Saffron has a bitter taste. When you, the beloved, allow the life of Perfect Love to live in you, the result is a fragrance that your life exudes, and it fills the atmosphere every place you go and every heart you touch. You have identified with Him through suffering and have tasted the saffron in your own life, allowing it to release a fragrance from your life that represents heaven on earth.

He goes on to describe the Shulamite as a garden with "calamus and cinnamon." Calamus is another fragrance used for perfume that is extremely sweet aroma. Cinnamon and calamus mixed together depict a very sweet yet spicy aroma. These aromas awaken the senses of those around them. Your life's fragrance leaves impressions on others and awakens their hearts because you are a garden belonging to Him and this garden is filled with special aroma, spices, and fruit like no other.

Your garden is described as trees of frankincense. When your life is planted in this garden, you become trees of righteousness, as spoken of in Isaiah 61:3. Frankincense is a resin taken from the very hardy Boswellia tree by slashing the bark (stripping), which allows the resins to bleed out and harden. The hardened resins are called *tears*. Boswellia sacra trees, where the frankincense is derived, grow in very unforgiving conditions, sometimes even out of solid rock. The more hardy the condition where they grow, the more fragrant the aroma of tears. The resin is aromatic and used as incense and perfume. It is one of the special gifts given to Christ at his birth; it represents His deity. If our lives are symbolic of the Boswellia tree, then the harder the condition, the greater quality of fragrance there is because our dependence upon the Beloved becomes greater and He promises to turn ashes into beauty.

The Beloved experienced the degree of stripping that no man has endured when He was whipped and slashed so we could have healing and life. He endured this pain for all mankind. I would like to think that the tear formed from the frankincense resin is symbolically shouting, "This is what your Beloved went through in the garden of Gethsemane, crying tears of anguish and joy with you always on His mind." Only a man with deity in Him could accomplish such a sacrificial expression of Perfect Love.

Myrrh and aloes are the last incense and perfumes to describe your life's garden. Aloes are ointments used to treat wounds. You have all that you need to care for others in the garden the Beloved has specially picked for your life. Myrrh is also a resin that a tree bleeds when it is pierced or wounded through the bark and into the sapwood. Myrrh was another gift given to the Christ child at His birth. Myrrh is used as a perfume in burial preparation and was equal in weight value to gold in ancient history. The Beloved's body was covered with myrrh at His burial. It serves as perfumed ointment in preserving the body. Because of His sacrificial love for you, His beloved, you are covered in something even more perfect and pure than myrrh—His shed blood. When He looks at you, He sees you spotless because of His covering over your life. Will you share what you have found in your garden with others? All you need is found in your garden because it contains all the chief spices.

A fountain of gardens represents the planting and multiplication you accomplish by helping others' lives as a result of tending to what you already have. You are able to be fruitful and pour into others' gardens (lives) as you have faithfully tended to your garden through His direction. Your life is a place where others can grow in Him and plant in good soil all things specially designed for their life. Multiplication of goodness and love is taking place in your life as seen in the lives you touch with His love. Their identity can begin to come forth just as yours has, and they will begin to see themselves as a reflection of the Beloved because love has touched their heart through your life (garden).

There is an overflowing well of living waters and streams from Lebanon that flow out of the beloved now because her true authority and identity is found in the Beloved. She believes what He sees and says about her, and she believes what He says she can accomplish through love. The Beloved has gone before her and shown the perfect path. He has been faithful to help her tend to the garden of her life, pulling the weeds that are replaced with pleasant fragrance, incense, fruitfulness, and spices that is only possible because her identity is hidden in His.

Mount Hermon is the highest peak in Lebanon and is capped with white snow. Streams from Mount Hermon flow out washing the land, providing refreshing waters for growth and cultivation, and watering the region below. Do streams of living water flow out of your life watering others? There are many people with lives like a parched garden. They are waiting for a beloved like you to water them.

At the end of chapter four, the Shulamite responds in verse 16 saying, "Awake, O north wind, and come, O south! Blow upon my garden that its spices may flow out. Let my Beloved come to His garden and eat its pleasant fruits." The Shulamite is inviting Him to bring what is necessary for her life to depict righteousness, holiness, obedience, and love, reflecting the Beloved. She wants to be like Him and knows He will allow the north winds of adversity to purify but will also bring south winds of blessings and grace to comfort with strength, endurance, and rest. The cry of her heart is to be more like her Beloved. He calls her His beloved, and she is believing what He says about her. He has proven Himself and paved a way through His actions of sacrificial love. He has spoken to her heart at every turn of her journey even when she didn't even realize He was there and speaking. He has never left her nor will He ever.

She is perfect, spotless, and blameless in His eyes. He cannot forsake a love like His own.

Do you know He never gave up on you even when you turned your back on Him, looking for other things to satisfy you? He is faithful and true. He hedges you in and behind. He saves you from not only your enemies, but yourself. Your heart is not pure like His, but He is continually transforming it to be more like His. Yet, He still calls you beautiful and lovely. He still calls you His beloved. This is true love. Your soul can sit down in peace because of the assurance of His love. He is your resting place and high tower. The place you run into when chased by the enemy of your soul.

Many will abandon you, but not Him. You are His love. He is steady and will stay the course with you. Your destiny fulfilled is His purpose. He says you are elegant and extravagant, and He is enamored with your beauty. He sees your limited love, but He also sees your desire for Him, and that compels Him and draws Him even closer to you. Who can quench the love He has for you? Nothing can stand in the way of His love and your love. The rhythm of this perfectly synchronized dance moves with an ease and grace. Authority, compassion, provision, identity, value, destiny, beauty and strength are the beloveds as she follows habitually in the lovesick dance with her Beloved, Jesus. Let the dance begin!

Prayer: Beloved, help me to keep my gaze upon you. My understanding of who I am, my authority, destiny and how much you love me has been limited. I'm beginning to see more clearly the lies I have believed about myself. I am ready to know the truth and to follow you in my journey. I believe the dance between you and I can be perfectly synchronized rhythm and I am ready to begin. In Jesus's name, Amen.

Love's Delayed Response

I have come to my garden, my sister, my spouse; I have gathered my myrrh with my spice; I have eaten my honeycomb with my honey; I have drunk my wine with my milk. Eat, O friends? Drink, yes, drink deeply, O beloved ones? I sleep, but my heart is awake; it is the voice of my beloved! He knocks, saying, "Open for me, my sister, my love, my dove, my perfect one. For my head is covered with dew, My locks with the drops of the night." I have taken off my robe; how can I put it on again? I have washed my feet; how can I defile them? My beloved put his hand by the latch of the door, and my heart yearned for him. I arose to open for my beloved, and my hands dripped with myrrh, my fingers with liquid myrrh, on the handles of the lock. I opened for my beloved but my beloved had turned away and was gone. My heart leaped up when he spoke. I sought him, but I could not find him; I called him, but he gave me no answer. The watchmen who went about the city found me. They struck me, they wounded me; the keepers of the walls took my veil away from me. I charge you, O daughters of

Jerusalem, if you find my beloved, that you tell him I am lovesick!

—Song of Solomon 5:1–8

In Song of Solomon 5:1, the Beloved is declaring He has come to engage closer with the Shulamite. His desire is to draw closer, and He expresses all the beautiful qualities her heart is showing when He speaks of the myrrh and spice, honeycomb and honey, and wine with milk. Her life (heart) is fruitful, and she has made room for the Beloved to enjoy her life. He calls for others to enjoy being with her as He does, knowing that others will benefit from the fruitfulness of her life. He loves her presence. Although, at the moment, His desire to be closer is stronger than her desire for His presence, as seen in the verses that follow.

The Shulamite wants to be closer to the Beloved and is not content staying at this depth of love in their relationship, but her heart is troubled because of her delayed response when the Beloved comes, as stated in verse 6. She responds but not quickly enough because he is gone when she finally goes to open the door. It is true she wants more intimacy with him; the Beloved knows the condition of her heart, and He knows drawing away from her is best for their relationship because it will compel her to seek Him out responsively. Christ promises to never leave us or forsake us. His presence is always with us whether we feel it or acknowledge it. But there are times we take for granted

His sweet presence that He so lovingly and freely lavishes upon us. When we don't respond quickly, He does what is needed to draw us closer: He draws away. Yet this removal of His presence is only to get our attention. We begin to realize how desperate we are without Him close. We realize we cannot camp out where He left us. We must follow and pursue Him just as the children of Israel followed the cloud by day and the fire by night. He pursued her, but she hesitated to respond. This hesitation cost her His presence, but not His continued protection. As she begins to seek where He has gone, she encounters some elders or those in authority. They ridicule or chastise her for her lovesick actions in pursuit of Him. How many times are we expected or encouraged to tone down our lovesick heart, the expression of this love, and the driven pursuit to encounter His love and presence deeper? Are we willing to run after him relentlessly no matter what the cost? Are we willing to be made a fool of and be ridiculed for our exposed lovesick heart and the openness we portray of our love's expression?

Maybe you have never responded to the Beloved's knock at the door of your heart. Maybe you have responded, but you realize He wants to experience a deeper relationship with you, but you have ignored the knock or made excuses not to respond. Are you too busy with the cares of life to be still long enough and feel His tug on your heartstrings? Don't allow any more excuses to be made. Trust that Perfect

Love has found you and He is ready to impart His love into your heart.

> *Prayer:* Beloved, I need you close to me at all times. Forgive me when you have tugged at my heart strings and I have not responded quickly enough, or ever at all. I am responding to your love now. My heart is open to receive all the fullness of your love. I have delayed responding long enough. I need your presence in my life. In Jesus's name, Amen.

Draw Me Away with You

January, 2011 I spent time in Fredericksburg, Texas, at a bed and breakfast called Angels Lodge Above the Creek while on sabbatical. I experienced something incredible during my time away that showed me coming to this place was such a divine purpose and direction by God. I noticed a small statue of an angel hidden under the windmill on the property while out walking. It was early morning and I was taking pictures of the sunrise and the creek when I stumbled upon this beautiful statue hidden away under the windmill. But the sweetest thing about this angel is the plaque that had Song of Solomon 3:4 written upon it! I knew then my next topic for the book would be based on Song of Solomon 3:4. I also knew that after reading this Scripture that my drawing away with the Beloved eight beautiful days delighted Him so much, and my pursuit of Him would bring the Beloved closer to my heart. This time has been invaluable and one of the best investments I have ever made.

> Scarcely had I passed by them, when I found the one I love. I held Him and would not let Him go until I had

brought Him to the house of my mother, and into the chamber of her who conceived me.

—Song of Solomon 3:4

Men and women do think differently to some degree, but when it comes to desiring to spend quality time with the person you absolutely adore, they are definitely the same. When love captures your heart, you give much of your time thinking of that special someone. Think for a moment how the Beloved feels. The same, except exaggerated ten times! He is Perfect Love. When our hearts turn toward Him throughout our day or night, it excites His heart, and He is there to listen. The Beloved is always ready to hear our conversation and adoration, and is even there to listen to our grumbles and complaints. We may not be able to see the Beloved with our natural eye (although I have heard stories from saints who have had encounters with Him), but we certainly *sense* and *feel* His presence, love, and adoration for us when we take the time to draw close to Him. Any movement toward the Beloved moves His heart and compels Him to draw closer to you, His beloved. A glance in His direction is special to Him. A gaze in His direction and you become a reflection of His perfect love.

Do you remember your honeymoon or a getaway with someone you love and adore? Do you remember a spontaneous, spur-of-the-moment choice to go somewhere you have never been with the one you love? These times will always be remembered and cherished as special beyond words. That is exactly what the Beloved thinks when you want to run away somewhere special with Him. It may be in your own home for a few minutes, or it may be long trips like the one I described above. Whichever He leads you to do, I can assure you the time you spend together will do things for you and for Him that only the special moment can express the fullness of that time. There will be understanding, love, and revelation imparted to you that is worth all the gold in the world. It will be priceless and will carry you through difficult times. His heart longs to adorn you with grace and beauty when you draw away with Him. He is waiting to encounter you at the depths of your heart. Will you make the time when He is tugging on your heartstrings?

The following are some very special moments when I have made the choice to draw away with the Beloved. I want to share them with you and stir up your desire to do the same. He will do for you what He has done for me. Just take the time.

SEPTEMBER 4, 2011

A few days ago while driving to church, I began to go over in my mind the things that needed to be done and concerns of my heart. There were many decisions that would need to be made by the end of the year, and I was pondering these decisions. It dawned on me that if I were married, I would be discussing these things with my spouse, and then my focus went to Jesus. I felt as though he was listening and pondering with me as I was thinking. It was one of those moments when the reality of His sweet concern and presence in your life is so real. I smiled and began to talk out loud about some of the things I was pondering. The closeness I share with Him is worth all the years of being alone. For me, Jesus allowed this alone time so that an intimacy with Him would develop and would not be focused on a husband, but only Him. I would not trade these years for anything. He is so excited to spend time with us when He calls us to come away. We really have no true idea of how excited He gets just thinking about us. He can't wait to talk with us, ponder with us, meditate with us, laugh with us, dance with us, and just be with His sweet companion.

> My beloved spoke, and said to me: "Rise up, my love, my fair one, and come away. For lo, the winter is past, the rain is over and gone. The flowers appear on the earth; the time of singing has come, and the voice of the turtledove is heard in our land. The fig tree puts forth her green figs, and the vines with the tender grapes give a good smell. Rise up, my love, my fair one, and come away!"
>
> —Song of Solomon 2:10–14

Personal Vision

I had come home from prayer on Thursday night. It was the fall of 2009. Tracy, a sweet friend of mine, had been speaking on the Father, Son, and Holy Spirit and their ministry to us, and that the three are one. It was late at night, and I was tired so I left a little early. As I got into my car, I had the thought that I wanted the Lord to download to me what He was teaching that night even though I did not stay in the meeting. I did not even verbally sound out my prayer but quietly thought it in my mind. To my surprise, He did exactly that. As I lay down on my bed that night, I immediately had a vision of Jesus elevated slightly above me. His legs were crossed, and He sat there with a smile on His face looking at me, running his fingers of one hand in a motion like you do when you want to say something. It was so very real, and He was acting so normal. Then He said to me, "I have missed our time together." My heart was listening. Then I saw Him look upward to the Father who was also nearby. The Father was a ray of light that was beaming. I did not see the Father's face but only saw His glorious radiance. As He was looking at the Father, Jesus said, "Father, isn't she beautiful and don't you love to see her dance?" The Father said "Yes, My Son, I know. I created her that way." Jesus had the biggest smile on His face, and I heard both of them just chuckle. Then Jesus looked straight into me and spoke to the Holy Spirit inside of me and said "Holy Spirit, what do you think?" And the Holy Spirit said, "I like being here!" He said it with such delight and pleasure, like He would rather not be anywhere else.

I began to laugh, and this incredible peace and presence of God filled my room. I saw all this happening before me and could hardly believe I was listening in on a conversation that the three were having about simple me! I said out loud, "I cannot believe this is happening! Jesus, is that really you?" I laughed. "You know, if anyone saw me or heard what I was saying, they would think I was crazy!" They stayed a few more minutes and then left me with such a sense of their love, acceptance, delight, and pleasure over me.

I wanted to share this vision to encourage each and every person reading these pages. I can assure you that God gave me this vision not because I have been such a great and wonderful person or Christian and deserve such love and encouragement. That's not at all the reason. It has everything to do with His incredible, devoted love and affection for me and all of us. He has no favorites but wants to make each of us feel and think we are His favorite. Whoa, how He sweetly does this is profound!

The only reason He revealed such tenderness and His delight over me that night was simply because He loves me and He knew I needed encouragement. When you are engaged to be married, your loved one does not stop telling you how much they love you and adore you. Neither does God, who is the lover of our soul. He made us and knows our weaknesses and strengths. He knows we need to be reminded of His endearing love by bringing His sweet presence into our life continually. *It has nothing to do with how good or bad a Christian we are.* It has everything to do with how much He loves us and delights in us!

> ***Prayer:*** Beloved, I believe your love is real and tangible. I realize my need to draw away with you. I also know my need for your encouragement to get through life. I want to hear what you have to say about me. Speak to me through your Scriptures, a dream, vision, or the still small voice. Speak to me any way you want. I am ready and open to receive your thoughts concerning me. In Jesus's name, Amen.

Beauty for Ashes

> Do not look upon me, because I am dark, because the sun has tanned me. My mother's sons were angry with me; they made me the keeper of the vineyards, but my own vineyards I have not kept.
>
> —Song of Solomon 1:6

Many of you reading this book have experienced much hardship, trauma, and chaos in your lives. Many of you can relate to the Shulamite's description of her own soul when she describes it as dark. Her soul has been wounded from past experiences, in addition to her own crippling choices. I was born into chaos, yet in all of it, God was in control of my life even when I did not know it. All men are broken, and broken men break their children, and they grow up to be a broken man, but God is bigger than that. Even the best of earthly fathers leave bruises behind, but God is not like our earthly fathers. And we are not like our earthly fathers as God breaks the mold and transforms these earthen broken vessels into beautiful cisterns that are full of sweet-smelling oil. The oil and aroma of your life pours out onto everyone you meet, touches the brokenness in their lives, and heals. On and on this legacy continues.

Not only do we receive brokenness from our fathers or mothers, but we also receive wounds from our past experiences with others or from life difficulties. Old wounds will continue to reopen with every hurtful experience we encounter that is similar to our past wounds. We must be willing to receive healing from old wounds for us to respond in healthy ways to new experiences, whether pleasant or not. These wounds often are the reason we make unhealthy choices. Put in another way, if we consider our souls as a full glass of water and the water becomes darkened by debris, we do not filter our thoughts through a clear, healed perspective of the soul. The darkened soul will then make choices and receive perspective that is not clear, healed, or guided by truth, making our decisions and reactions wrong many times. Once the wounds are healed, it is easier to see things clear and from a healthy perspective, which allows us to respond to life and others in a healthy way, including our response to the Heavenly Father. We will begin to see His love for us clearer than ever before, and instead of just head knowledge of His love, we will have revelations from the heart of His love. How many times have you thought you *knew* God loved you but you did not *feel* God's love? When you receive the heart revelation with the head knowledge of His love because you have been healed of past wounds, then you will truly feel and know His love for you.

The dark night of the soul can be a profound place where the wounds surface. We experience these dark seasons not because God is a mean father and he doesn't care about His children. On the contrary, it is because He loves us so very much that He saves us from ourselves and from the false luxury of not knowing these dark times. It is in these times that what is hidden in the dark truly comes to the light if we will allow it to. It is true that light shines much brighter in the darkness. The light of truth and His healing will shine brighter during the times when the soul is the darkest. You may even call these times a journey in the wilderness. You may feel and think that the Father has left you in this dark place, but He has not left you. He only wants to penetrate His healing light and truth in the dark places so you can soar on the mountaintop and leave the valley. You must say yes to the north wind blowing on your soul. As you abide and allow the light to be shed on the dark places and wounds of your soul, the south wind will bring comfort and healing. As the Shulamite says in the Song of Solomon 4:16, "Awake, O north wind, and come, O south! Blow upon my garden, that its spices may flow out. Let my beloved come to His garden and eat its pleasant fruit." The garden is your life, and the spices that flow out are all your thoughts, decisions, actions, and understanding responding to your life. He comes to your life and partakes of the pleasant fruit of your life as you have been willing to allow His light to shine on the wounds. The pleasant fruit is also a result of the obedient choices and faithful heart you have sought after at any price.

> ***Prayer:*** Heavenly Father, I am truly your child. I have knowledge of your love from your Word, but I have failed to feel your love for me. I need to know and to feel your love, so I give you permission to shed your light on any wounds in my heart and bring healing. I realize from these wounds I have believed lies the enemy would have me believe because I was in a dark place, but I pray for your perspective and truth to be shed on these wounds (experiences, trauma). You transcend time, so you can tell me or show me your truth in each one of these experiences. You were there all the time; I just did not know you were or feel your presence during these dark times. I invite you to bring your healing to each experience and wound. I want my soul to be clear, whole, and healed so I can not only know your love but feel it. I want your truth to prevail in my thoughts; I want your perspective. No longer do I want lies to veil the truth about my identity, worth, and value. I know this will only make my relating to you more wonderful and my relationships with others powerful as well. Thank you for healing me because you love me more than I can comprehend. In Jesus's precious name, AMEN.

A Time of Waiting

> Have you not known? Have you not heard? The everlasting God, the Lord, the Creator of the ends of the earth, neither faints nor is weary. His understanding is unsearchable. He gives power to the weak and to those who have no might, He increases strength. Even the youths shall faint and be weary, and the young men shall utterly fall, but they that "wait" upon the Lord shall renew their strength. They shall mount up with wings as eagles. They shall run and not be weary. They shall walk and not faint.
>
> —Isaiah 40: 28–31

Have you ever observed a race horse in his shoot when the whistle is about to blow and the gate about to fling wide open? His eyes begin to change from mellow to alert. His body positions itself for the run of his life with intensity. He feels the excitement, and the strength of that excitement exudes from him overflowing to his rider. He was born to run. He was born to win. In many ways, the picture of this elegant creature of such endurance is a replica of who we are. When we begin to gaze upon our Lord and Savior and embrace all that He has died for us to have, we want to run with endurance the race set before us. We want to set out on our journey to fulfill our destiny. Have you asked yourself why it is taking so very long? The waiting is almost excruciating and painful at times.

What comes out of this time of pressing in and enduring? His promises to us in waiting are seen in Isaiah 40:28–31. One of the promises is strength to run and not grow weary. Seasons of waiting produce strength of character to sustain what is ahead. This means that hope deferred most likely will find a place in your heart while enduring and persevering in the wait. Hope deferred and discouragement are like speaking barriers that scream loudly to "give up" or "it's taking too long." Many times right before you cross your finish line in whatever you are waiting for, there is pain with lots of hope deferred and discouragement. Sometimes these barriers come several times throughout the entire journey. But how do you endure this waiting?

Perseverance, *endurance*, and *steadfastness* are words with such powerful meanings. Have you ever waited for something that took years to manifest and obtain? If you have, then I know you have experienced hope deferred. In fact, hope deferred is part of your strengthening process. So before you throw this book out the window for that statement, follow my train of thought for a moment! Waiting! Waiting for unfulfilled promises! Waiting for your purpose to be fulfilled. We live in a generation where waiting is uncomfortable. Instant promises, instant spouses, instant jobs, instant ministries, instant prayers answered—these are the things we desire, and time becomes an unwelcomed source. We definitely live in a fast-paced, give-it-to-me-now-or-I'll-make-it-happen generation. Sometimes God calls you to wait beyond what you think you can bare. Our souls cry out, "Why?" in the waiting. You hear His voice tell you in this quiet place that it is well with your soul. His sufficiency is what girds you and sustains you. Waiting can produce endurance, perseverance, and steadfastness if you allow it to have its way in you. Many times your response to Him is, "No, it is not well with my soul." But truly He sees the very moment and the outcome, and He knows you better than you know yourself. At the point of discomfort, you have a critical choice to make. You can choose to stay in your discouragement and hope deferred, or you can admit you are about to give up and desperately need Him to come to the rescue. You can be honest and have a heart-to-heart conversation with Him. He already knows what is in your heart, so you might as well be honest. His help may take on different forms. A friend may speak words of wisdom to you at just the right time. It may be to seek wise counsel from someone or admit to those around you how discouraged you feel and in need of specific prayer for a season. It may be redirection for your life. It may mean laying down what you think is the right focus and purpose, considering a completely different path. Sometimes roadblocks are actually the Father's redirection. But you will only know by submitting yourself to His agenda for you and admitting you need help. The above are all part of enduring and persevering in the wait.

Focus your heart on the present, the moment-by-moment goodness of God. You are beginning to see your purpose and feel His love. This inspires you and encourages you to run and run hard. You think you are ready, and in many ways, you are prepared. But His timing is perfect. Be *thankful* for what has already happened and what has been provided for you along the way. A thankful heart gets you back to the right perspective. Remember chapter one? The moment by moment can be difficult but also surprising and enjoyable. He has not forgotten about you. He just knows you better than you know yourself; therefore, trust Him for the completion of all things in your life. If you get impatient and run ahead of Him, you may birth an Ishmael, and even though Ishmael had a promise from God and was blessed, it was not God's best and first choice. Genesis 17 reveals that the birth of Isaac was God's first choice to bring forth an everlasting covenant for future generations, but Sarah and Abraham were not willing to wait long enough. If you have birthed an Ishmael, as we most all do and have at times, it will work out for good. That is a promise He has made to us according to Romans 8:28, which says, "And we know that all things work together for good to those who love God, to those who are the called according to His purpose." So take your journey one step at a time. Be joyful in the moments that He gives you with a thankful heart. Focus your heart on the special moments in time along the way, and savor each moment so that the joy in the journey will not get lost in focusing solely on the end result of your destiny. You wonder why you feel burned out and your joy has been zapped and fried of all desire and fun! One most important reason is that *your focus is entirely on the end result and you forget to enjoy the moments in the journey along the way*.

Take an inventory right now of your life and become aware of this present moment. I'm sure if you stay there long enough, you will sense lots of goodness and many joyful things to be thankful for. Let your mind take a mental reprieve from the hurry of the race. Of course, stay on the path and continue to run the race, but look at the special encounters and savor each one as you are running. Don't be in a race against time itself. You will always lose that kind of race. The Father knows exactly when and how fast your pace needs to be, and there are so many wonderful things about your life He wants to speak to you about and use in extraordinary and simple ways. He wants you to experience the fullness of each experience, not just rush through them and say "next." Your life has far greater value than such a rushed, unnoticed mentality.

I recently trained for a half marathon. A half marathon is 13.1 miles. It took me approximately four months of consistent training to achieve this goal. I have always loved to run and did a lot of running in my younger days but had never run a half marathon. It has been a desire in my heart for probably twenty plus years. Being physically active has always been a part of my life, so beginning to train for this half marathon seemed possibly feasible, but let me strongly emphasize the word *possibly*. But I was determined. The desire was there, and I believe many good desires we have are unnoticeably inspired from the Heavenly Father. Some desires are more obvious from Him, and some are not so obvious. I remember the training process well.

A friend of mine who had run a few marathons asked me how the training was going in the beginning of the process. As I told them how far I was able to run and not stop, their response was not so positive. In fact, I detected the doubt in their mind that I would accomplish my goal of 13.1 miles in four months. I had a choice to make at that moment. I could choose to listen to the thought of doubt that was trying to plant itself, or I could listen to what I believe God thought about my progress. It left me with even more determination to accomplish my goal. Every week during the training, I had a goal to accomplish. Some weeks were better than others. I was met with pain and discomfort, but the discipline it took to train and press through the discomfort taught me much about our spiritual journey. Our journey with the Beloved is not always easy, but at every turn and encounter, you gain more resilience, trust, and grace to continue. Wisdom and strength set in, and now you have specific times of overcoming and enduring that you can remember to help propel you to the next place in your journey.

The day of the race comes. I had done my best in preparing. I felt physically, mentally, and spiritually ready for the run. I was not alone. Not only was my Beloved with me, but my precious daughter and two daughter-in-laws ran with me. My two sons were stationed at different intervals along the way to encourage us to finish. It was one of the greatest experiences I have ever had. Even in the pain of the last four miles, when my body was aching and my feet felt like they were going to fall off, there was pain and joy that I was about to finish with the people who love me the most. Joy and pain are such a mixture of emotions. The ones that love me most stayed with me all the way. In your journey, you have those close to you who will stay with you and encourage you, who love you and want to see you accomplish your goal, and who will be with you during your journey. You are not alone, and if you feel that way, ask God to connect you with the right people that will help you in your journey.

There is also help that is less obvious visually. Hebrews 12:1 speaks of this unseen help:

> Therefore we also, since we are surrounded by so great a cloud of witnesses, let us lay aside every weight, and the sin which so easily ensnares us, and let us run with endurance the race that is set before us, looking unto Jesus, the author and finisher of our faith, who for the joy that was set before Him endured the cross, despising the shame, and has sat down at the right hand of the throne of God.

You have loved ones, angels, and the Holy Spirit. You are not alone, and all eyes are on you to see that you endure and accomplish your destiny.

Isaiah 40:31 says, "But those who wait on the Lord shall renew their strength; they shall mount up with wings like eagles, they shall run and not be weary, they shall walk and not faint." An eagle's wings are aerodynamically perfect in the way they are made in order to help the eagle soar and glide. An eagle's wings are made perfect to catch the wind at the right position to soar and glide with as little energy exerted as possible. This enables the eagle to conserve the energy as he flies, giving him more energy to focus on his purpose. Do you prefer your journey to be filled with times of soaring and gliding, or expending lots of physical and emotional effort that burns you out quickly? The Holy

Spirit in your life is like a wind. Your identity, purpose, and destiny are determined, and the Father's perspective of you is essential to accomplishing every step in your journey. When you are aerodynamically positioned correctly with the Holy Spirit, you will be propelled to soar and glide. Grace and strength become your welcomed companions. You have heard the expression "catch the wave" when people surf. The same is true for soaring and gliding. You must catch the wind, or better yet, let it catch you.

To accomplish your journey on your own and with a mind-set that you can do it all yourself is surely a setup for failure. We are not islands, and it is important for us to recognize our need for something to help us that is greater than ourselves. In this place of humility, you admit your need to trust the help the Heavenly Father has provided, which is the Holy Spirit. Be still, wait, listen, and fill your heart with what His Word says about you. Before David ever went out to battle or any time he needed direction or understanding, he sought the Heavenly Father's wisdom. We should do the same. You will for sure soar to new heights and glide with new ease. It makes your journey much easier when difficulties come. This reassures you that you are not alone and will accomplish all that has been determined for your life. You are His beloved, and you are destined to succeed.

> ***Prayer:*** Heavenly Father, just as you gave the Beloved all that He needed to overcome, endure the pain, and

soar, I know you will do the same for me. I want to run the race that is set before me to fulfill my destiny, but the waiting has caused hope deferred. I want to give up in many ways. Holy Spirit, you are the one the Beloved has left with me to give me strength. Come be the wind that will give me strength to not give up, but to soar. In Jesus's name, Amen.

Catch Us the Little Foxes

> Catch us the foxes, the little foxes that spoil the vines, for our vines have tender grapes. My beloved is mine, and I am his. He feeds his flock among the lilies. Until the day breaks and the shadows flee away, turn, my beloved, and be like a gazelle or a young stag upon the mountains of Bether.
>
> —Song of Solomon 2:15–17

As you travel on this beautiful journey in uncharted territory, you will surely encounter temptations, accusations, emotional upheavals, downfalls, wrong turns, and a broken heart or two. Although these encounters are inevitable in a fallen world like ours, you will also encounter the beautiful presence and blessings that only come from a true love like Jesus.

Have you ever watched a little child who was unaware at what danger or harm they were about to experience? Their awareness of the dangers in their environment is undeveloped and immature. A parent's job is to protect and direct their child through teaching, discipline, and being an example. The Heavenly Father's desire is to protect and direct us through teaching and discipline. His Son is our living example, and His Word is our map. I want you to imagine for a moment that you are on a smooth dirt road. It is dirt instead of pavement because it is a road of humility that when chosen leads to honor. Along the sides of the road, there are rows and rows of large oak trees, and under the shadow of the large oak trees are the smaller oaks growing strong and tall like their examples that stand firm and strong beside them. These trees are planted in good soil and represent the people we will encounter along the way who are planted firmly in God's love. There are little plants and beautiful flowers planted as well of all variety. But with the bouquet of little plants and flowers, there also grows the weeds beside these wanting to choke them out. The plants and flowers represent others who are young and undeveloped in their journey. They are immature in their development and are in need of protection. As you walk along your path, you are very aware of the tender fruit growing: the grapes, apples, and berries. Lurking around the tall magnificent oak trees, the small immature trees, and all the tender undeveloped fruit and flowers are the foxes. Little foxes and big foxes. You can't help but look at them as you see them scamper here and there, taking what they want from the immature growth along the path. You look at them in amazement, noticing their beauty. The little foxes are so adorable. They get your attention, and you become very aware of their swiftness. You are certainly distracted and not sure what to do with them. They appear harmless and cute, but they are eating the tender growth before it can be fully developed, and destroying all the labor and growth of the precious plants and flowers. Do you stand by and watch this happen? They appear so cute and harmless! And who on earth could possibly catch the swift little critters? So you admire them for a time, but all the while, one by one they begin to devour the beauty in the landscape that your road is laced with.

What are these foxes along your journey? Are they hidden desires that contaminate you? Are they wounded places that have never been healed? Are they temptations that you give in to over and over again…the same ones? Are they generational propensities that seem to grip your every turn no matter what you do? Whatever they are, try and recognize them. List them out and give them to Lord. Find those you trust, the strong oaks, to pray for you. As you walk along this journey, there is a beautiful growth taking place. This growth needs an opportunity to mature. The foxes must be dealt with no matter how comfortable and cute they may appear to be. They are truly devouring the very beauty that your journey is laced with.

Do you remember how wonderful you thought everything was flowing between you and your special someone—no major issues and everything almost seemed too good to be true? Our love encounter and relationship with Jesus is much the same. He comes to our garden, which He has planted and developed, nurtured, and watered. He tenderly pursues us in our garden, showing us the weeds that need pulling and good things that need to be planted. We willingly allow Him in. And just when everything seems perfect, we suddenly say, "What just hit me?" Precious child of God, it was a "little fox," which seemed so harmless that came to disrupt this beautiful garden Jesus has so tenderly and lovingly cared for—your precious life!

You see the foxes come out in full force in the springtime when all is in full bloom and flourishing, when all seems perfect and wonderful. They love to disrupt by eating things in our garden that should not be eaten—the tender grapes, the new fruit in our lives that has just begun to grow into luscious fruit, mature, and abundant. They dig holes in the garden that should not be dug. They disrupt the peace and pleasantness of the garden in a way that is subtle and unexpected. But they are so cute and little, looking very harmless, so we don't pay much attention to them and let them continue. They disrupt your relationship with Jesus; they disrupt the sweet communion. They will also interfere with other close relationships—family and friends. These distractions that look so harmless, or not that important, actually can destroy your garden and leave devastation. What are they and what do they look like. Everyone's little foxes can look a little different. Unhealthy relationships or desires, worldliness, lust of the flesh, idols, or anything that seems to bring temporary satisfaction outside of Him. The cute little foxes grow into big foxes.

Discerning the things in our lives that are distractions and allowing them to continue can be detrimental to our destiny. God is sovereign and in control, but the enemy of our souls would like nothing better than to sidetrack us. The Beloved will faithfully remain with us and bring to us healing and restoration, but the pain we go through can be avoided at times. The Scripture tells us to "catch us the little foxes that spoil the vines." That means that the little foxes are going to come into all our lives, but we are encouraged to catch them. Trials, tribulations, and temptations will come to all of us to refine and purify our lives. But how will we respond? What will be our choice and attitude? If our initial response is not right, how quickly will we admit we are weak and need the help of Him who loves us more than we can even imagine? Sometimes, the best prayer you can pray is "Lord, save me from myself."

"Until the day breaks and the shadows flee away" speaks of a soul in darkness, a soul in need of the morning light to break through, a soul desperate to eliminate the shadows of the past and all the pain that comes with the shadows. The Shulamite cries out for the Beloved to come in strength and power, grace and swiftness like a gazelle or young stag upon the mountains in her life that are too huge for her to conquer. She is admitting to her need for His strength, love, power, and grace to overcome the mountains that have caused a separation, a separation not only from Him but from who she really is and her destiny. She needs to be rescued from it all. The world would say she is weak if she can't do it herself. But Love says, "I'm here to empower you, transform you, encourage you, and fight your battles. As I do this for you, I will teach you my tactics of warfare and love. You will learn how to fight these battles, and we will do this together because My life is in you and you abide in Me." The Beloved knows that Love is what will connect them and sustain with power.

> ***Prayer:*** Heavenly Father, you know me better than I know myself. I admit my weaknesses to You, that I cannot overcome them. I'm in desperate need for you to deliver and heal my soul. I give you permission to shine the light on any and every chamber of my heart I have closed off. I want every room of my soul to be clean. Help me to be sensitive to *everything* you highlight no matter how small I may think it is. Highlight anything in my life that appears harmless but if left alone can cause devastation. Most of all, Father, save me from myself. In Jesus's precious name, AMEN.

A Seal Fashioned from Love and Covered in Grace

If I were to describe the heart's cry in all of this book of love, I would summarize it with Song of Solomon 8:7–8.

> Set me as a seal upon your heart, as a seal upon your arm; for love is as strong as death, jealousy as cruel as the grave; its flames are flames of fire, a most vehement flame. Many waters cannot quench love, nor can the floods drown it. If a man would give for love all the wealth of his house, it would be utterly despised.

The Beloved has won the heart and affection of His beloved. He has convinced her of His unfailing and unconditional faithfulness to only her through His love for her. His words and actions are congruent. As a result of His consistency, she is convinced of her own identity. She believes she is His beloved. She sees herself clearly the way He depicts her because the veil to her identity has been removed. He loved her into clarity of identity. Perfect Love does that. But her gaze was continuously upon Him. In Song of Solomon 8:7–8, they are both declaring the seal upon each other's hearts and arms. There is no amount of wealth that could buy her love or his—all other attempts would be despised. They have found each other and are the favorite in the eyes of the other one.

This is how your journey will be and hopefully has begun to be. Each beloved of the Beloved has a custom-made journey like none other. You were fashioned even in your mother's womb as Psalm 139 states. The Beloved knows you from the beginning to the end, and His love for you compels Him to seek you at every turn, attempting to capture your heart, hopefully successfully. He is relentless in His endeavor because the longing in His heart to be with you is stronger than any force created. He knows Perfect Love is the only ingredient that will convince you He is worthy to be yours and you are worthy to be His. After all, you reflect each other and the two of you are like one. Will you allow yourself to be loved so dearly and genuinely? Dare you give your heart to such Perfect Love? If you will lose yourself in Him, then you will be found!

When the seal of love is set upon these hearts and arms, nothing can separate the two. Out of the heart flows Perfect Love, and the arm representing authority yields to love and welcomes grace. Grace to continue in your journey becomes your best friend. Grace is your strength to endure and overcome. Love is what propels you to go on and on. A true beauty has a certain inner strength that is seen by all who come into contact with them. This inner strength that is so beautiful is the Beloved's glory that reflects upon you because you have been willing to gaze long enough throughout your journey on Perfect Love. You shine, beloved, with His glory. You choose not to stop in your journey and camp in one place but to continue on for the fullness of all available for you. Your destiny is secure, and your vision is clear. You dare not stop the race now. You have come too far to stop or turn back. Take a moment and reflect back to chapter 1 of Song of Solomon. In the beginning, the Shulamite sees herself as "dark" and asks the Beloved not to even look upon her. He begins to reassure her of how He sees her in chapter 1. The reassurance and encouragement of her identity continues throughout every chapter. We can see the veil to her identity being removed, allowing clarity and understanding to unfold. She becomes progressively more solid and certain from chapter 1 to 8 of who she is and her value to the Beloved. Song of Solomon 8:3–4 states, "His left hand is under my head, and his right hand embraces me. I charge you, O daughters of Jerusalem, do not stir up nor awaken love until it pleases." She declares how He has formed her identity with His embrace. She does not want to be disturbed because she has welcomed the process. In Song of Solomon 8:10 she calls herself a "wall," and says "then I became in his eyes as one who found peace." This verse means she has settled her own identity and is at peace with herself and the Beloved's love for her. Will you too embrace the process until the end, allowing Perfect Love to mold you?

Remember the race horse in the shoot? You have waited long enough. Now run! You are His beloved, now believe everything that He says about you. He has written you the most beautiful love song in the world as seen in the Song of Solomon. His banner over you is love. Most of us have always wanted a song written about us, and it has been there for hundreds of years. He was waiting for us to discover this song of love for His beloved.

I have encountered trials as everyone does; I have met and faced loneliness firsthand. I have experienced betrayal, ridicule, and rejection. Grief has gripped me a time or two. But out of it all, Perfect Love from my Beloved has swooped down and picked me up every single time. And through it all, I became more certain of who I am and why, where I am going, what my purpose is, and just how special I am to Him. I have experienced joy, security, and contentment worth more than all the riches of the world. I have felt deep love from the Father that refreshed and energized me to continue on my journey, giving me the grace and security to be steadfast and strong. There is a contentment in knowing you are loved by the dearest and best Father ever, your Creator and Heavenly Father. You are a reflection of His Beloved Son, Jesus. Will you dare to believe it? I do!

> ***Prayer:*** Heavenly Father, I have believed lies about me and who I am long enough. I know your Son's love song was written just for me. He is Perfect Love and the Beloved. I want to experience His love at a deeper level more than ever before. I want to feel His love daily and encounter Him in ways like never before. I want to understand my value, worth, identity, and destiny. Please come in all your love and capture my heart. I want to be more like you and reflect your Son everywhere I go, so help me set my gaze upon Him. Help me know the truth about who I am so that I can experience true life. I want to be a life giver and give away freely to others what you have given to me. You are showing me my destiny, and I am believing I am your beloved. In Jesus's name, Amen.